IMPERATRIX ÆTERNA

The following works are in the public domain:

From 'San Miniato' by Oscar Wilde, p. v.
'The Litany of the Seven Kisses' by Clark Ashton Smith, p. 15.
'Caeruli Oculi' by Théophile Gautier (translated by Agnes Lee), p. 23.
'The Secret Rose' by Clark Ashton Smith, p. 26.
From 'The New Helen' by Oscar Wilde, p. 33.
From 'Pan to Artemis' by Aleister Crowley, p. 44.
'Hymn' by Edgar Allen Poe, p. 50.
From 'To a Madonna' by Charles Baudelaire
(translated by Frank Pearce Sturm), p. 65.
'Song of the Stars in Praise of Her' by David Park Barnitz, p. 123.

First published in 2023.
Hadean Press Limited
Unit 30, Mantra House
South Street, Keighley
West Yorkshire
BD21 1SX
England
www.hadeanpress.com

IMPERATRIX ÆTERNA

Magical Stories
of the Queen of Heaven

by Pope St. Celestine V,
Charles Baudelaire, Aleister Crowley
and others

Translated and compiled by

Robert Nixon, OSB

And throned upon the crescent moon
The virginal white Queen of Grace,—
Mary! could I but see thy face
Death could not come at all too soon.
O crowned by God with thorns and pain!
Mother of Christ! O mystic wife!
My heart is weary of this life
And over-sad to sing again…

Oscar Wilde
from 'San Miniato'

CONTENTS

Noble Daughters of Mary
by Ippolito Marracci

TRANSLATOR'S INTRODUCTION

The veneration of a divine or quasi-divine feminine figure is a virtually omnipresent phenomenon in the various spiritual traditions of humankind. This phenomenon derives, at its most basic level, from the complex archetype of a mystical woman, a *Magna Mater*, vested with both power and compassion—and serving as the complement, refuge and *telos* of masculinity, and the *speculum*, idealization or apotheosis of femininity. This archetype is so primal as to transcend all the more particularized mythological systems, and to find a multitude of different expressions within each system.

Accordingly, Christianity, despite its monotheistic and patriarchal sources, very soon found it necessary to assume for itself a figure of the supernatural feminine in its cultic practice, in the form of the Blessed Virgin Mary. From a purely scholarly perspective, the multi-faceted figure of the Virgin Mary could readily be interpreted as an amalgam of Artemis, Hera, Athena, Aphrodite, and even Hekate, or any number of other primordial female deities. But, from the perspective of Faith, each of these supernatural women could equally be seen as mystically foreshadowing the various aspects and virtues of the unique Empress of the Angels. It goes without saying, of course, that the 'absolute truth' of the matter—the transcendent and ineffable reality which 'dwells in inaccessible light'—remains entirely and infinitely beyond any and all of the provisional symbols, names and avatars which point towards it.

The significance of the Blessed Virgin Mary in the spiritual heritage of Christianity, especially in the Roman Catholic and the Oriental and Eastern Orthodox traditions, can hardly be overstated. The devotion to this feminine figure has always been of particular prominence in the 'folk' or popular manifestations of these traditions, which have the freedom to respond to and express spiritual realities grasped spontaneously and instinctively. Indeed, the more intellectual and doctrinaire approaches to Christianity (such as those of Calvin and Luther) have often sought to moderate and restrain popular devotion to the Queen of Heaven, in some cases even identifying it as a form of 'crypto-Paganism'. Despite this, the spiritual potency of the Mother of Mercy is powerfully and consistently attested to by the *lex orandi*, and even people who feel little sympathy to the moral teachings or practices of the mainstream Church still retain confidence in the compassion and efficacy of the Blessed Virgin as a spiritual guide and helper.

The learned Johannes Trithemius avers that the Mother of God is "a more powerful spiritual helper to human beings than any and all other creatures in Heaven and on earth", and according to a well-known prayer attributed to St. Bernard of Clairvaux, "never was it known that anyone who fled to Her protection, implored Her help, or sought Her intercession was left unaided". In the context of such potent commendations, the contemporary spiritual practitioner can find no better or more powerful ally in their endeavours, regardless of their particular goals, beliefs, or backgrounds.

This volume presents two fascinating collections of short narratives which illustrate the potency, splendor and all-embracing compassion of the glorious Queen of Heaven in a wonderful fashion. The first is a collection of miracle stories written by the enigmatic and eccentric St. Celestine V (1215-1296). Celestine was a mysterious but highly charismatic hermit, who (despite being neither a bishop nor a cardinal) was elected to the papacy under bewildering and almost inexplicable circumstances in 1292. He was then forcibly deposed within five months of his election.[1] After taking secret flight from the Church authorities, Celestine was captured and held in strict isolation in a kind of 'ecclesiastical prison' for the remainder of his life. Despite this, the common people continued to venerate him as a great thaumaturge and a living saint, and he was canonized very shortly after his death.

His collection of miracles stories of the Virgin Mary contain rare and illuminating examples of 13th-century Italian 'folk-Catholicism'. The present translation is based on the text *De Miraculis Beatae Virginis Mariae*, included within the *S. Petri Caelestini PP. V Opuscula Omnia* published by Octavio Beltrani in Naples in 1640. In the majority of cases, the narrations provide a bare minimum (if any) context as to details of place or time, yet they are always infused with vivid color, dream-like vibrancy, and crystalline succinctness.

Despite the beauty of these stories, there is much that would seem to transgress the bounds of strict orthodoxy and conventional piety, and not a little that would make most Catholic theologians distinctly uncomfortable. Yet it is perhaps precisely where the stories become the most emphatically 'weird' that the mystery of the celestial Feminine is most touchingly and enchantingly illustrated.

The second collection is taken from *Heroides Mariana, seu de Illustrium Foeminarum Principum in Mariam Deiparem Virginem Pietate* ('Marian Heroines, or the Piety of Illustrious Noblewomen towards the Virgin Mary, the Mother of God') by Ippolito Marracci, first published in Rome in 1659. Marracci (1604-1675) was a priest of the Order of Clerics Regular of the Mother

---

1 Certain versions of the history of Celestine's pontificate indicate that his retirement was entirely voluntary, but given his subsequent period of flight and hiding, this seems unlikely.

of God, and a distinguished theologian and prolific author of works on Marian piety. This collection presents stories of noble women, including empresses, queens, princesses and countesses, who took the Mother of Mercy as their own special protector and helper. Some of the stories are quite conventional; but most are strange and wonderful, and not a few are fantastical and bizarre. Yet the very color and diversity of the narratives is a convincing testimony, if not necessarily to their objective truth, at least to the authenticity of the beloved traditions and legends which they encapsulate.

A number of short extracts from the relevant works of various poets (including Wilde, Clark Ashton Smith, Crowley, Poe, Baudelaire, and others) have been inserted at what seem like suitable junctures. It is intended that these brief poetic interludes will provide welcome opportunities for respite from the narrative movement, and moments of mystical reflection and contemplation.

It is the humble hope of the translator that these collections may be the source of wonder, diversion and inspiration, both for the scholar, the devotee, and the merely curious. And may the Queen of Heaven and the Empress of the Angels help us each to attain to whatever it is that our hearts most desire!

Robert Nixon, OSB,
Monk of the Abbey of the Most Holy Trinity, New Norcia

MIRACLES OF THE BLESSED VIRGIN

BY POPE ST. CELESTINE V

i. THE HAND OF A CERTAIN PRIEST IS AMPUTATED BY THE EMPEROR, AND RESTORED BY THE VIRGIN MOTHER OF GOD

A certain priest was once accused of having written a letter against the reigning Emperor; now this accusation was false, for he had not done so. Nevertheless a sentence was passed against him, that the hand with which he was alleged to have written the letter should be cut off. And very soon the gruesome sentence was carried out, with the severed hand being hung before the door of the church at which the accused priest ministered. Now it happened that this church was dedicated to the Blessed Virgin Mary.

With complete faith in Divine Providence, the priest humbly gave thanks to God for the misfortune and injustice which had befallen him. However he mourned in his heart that he was no longer capable of offering the sacrifice of the Holy Mass to the Lord. And so, feeling bitterly dejected, he approached an image of the Blessed Virgin in the church with his open wound on display, and exclaimed; "O Lady of Grace, is this the reward of all my labors? Is this the blessing due to your faithful servant? Indeed, my Queen, even if this is what was rightly due to me as punishment for my many failings, why have you permitted my hand to be cut off, the one instrument whereby I may best serve you? For many times that hand had written canticles in your praise, and many times it has offered to God the sacrifice of the Mass in your honor."

That night the priest, thoroughly exhausted, lay in his bed, neither fully asleep nor fully awake, when—behold!—the Blessed Virgin appeared before him. "What has happened to you, my son?" she said with tender compassion.

"I should ask *you*, my Lady," replied the priest tearfully, "where were you when all this was done to me? For the hand of your loving servant is now hanging before the door of this church!"

Mary replied to him, "Be comforted, my son. For the One who created human beings out of the void of nothingness is certainly able to restore your hand to you!" Saying this, she went through the church, and took down his severed hand from where it hung. She carefully placed it at the end of his wounded arm and it was restored immediately to perfect wholeness and function, as if it had never been cut off. Bidding the priest farewell, the Empress of the Angels then vanished into the air.

The next morning the priest arose, and in gratitude offered a solemn Mass in honor of the Blessed Virgin. And when the Emperor heard of these marvelous things, he rushed on foot to see the priest himself. Falling to his knees, he kissed the miraculously restored hand and humbly implored forgiveness for his error and cruelty.[2]

---

2 A variant of this story is told of St. John Damascene, who fell into conflict with the Byzantine emperor over the permissibility of sacred images—the emperor at the time sought to abolish the use of such images, whereas John strongly defended their use. Another variant of the story is told of Pope St. Leo the Great; in this version, it is Leo who severs his own hand, after becoming inflamed to lust when his hand was kissed by a devout woman. He later regretted this hasty action, and the Blessed Virgin restored his amputated hand to him.

ii. THE BLESSED VIRGIN, BY THE BALM OF THE MILK OF HER BOSOM, HEALS THE LIPS OF A CLERIC DEVOTED TO HER

There was once a certain cleric who would salute the Holy Mother of Christ with great regularity and sincere devotion. He would genuflect before her image and say a 'Hail Mary', as well as reciting the lines, "Blessed is the womb that bore the Savior of the world, and the breasts that suckled the Son of God!"

Now it happened that this cleric was suddenly afflicted by a terrible illness, so much so that the doctors despaired utterly of his chances of recovery. The pain grew so intense that he would gnaw at his own lips and tongue—and indeed, he would have eaten his whole body away had he been able to do so.

As he lay in his bed, in throes of dreadful agony and truly more dead than alive, he saw a certain person of incredible beauty appear at the end of his bead. He understood that this person, whose radiance was beyond that of mortals, was none other than his own guardian angel. This angel, with eyes turned towards Heaven, implored the Blessed Virgin Mary on behalf of the sick man: "What is this thing which has happened, O Queen of Mercy and font of piety?! Are these lips and this tongue, which I see to be so terribly injured, those same ones which so fervently praised and so passionately adored you? O Mistress of Angels and Empress of the stars, if you yourself do not help those devoted to you, who else will? Let it not be that pious hopes come to naught, or that those who seek refuge in you shall not find it!"

Then the Mother of God herself appeared to the sick man, and approaching closely, drew forth her sacred bosom from beneath her garments. And the same milk which had once nourished the infant Deity flowed forth freely into the mouth of the afflicted cleric. By virtue of this sacred balm, suddenly his lips and tongue were restored to full health, and his pain entirely taken away.

iii. THE BLESSED VIRGIN, REBUKING THE INFIDELITY OF ONE PLEDGED TO HER, SENDS HIM AWAY TO THE WILDERNESS

There was a young man who possessed a ring, which he had been given by a girlfriend of his. Between these two was a very natural bond of physical attraction, as is usual with young men and young women.

Now it was his custom to play in the church with the other young men, by kicking around a ball or indulging in other such sports. Once when he was doing so, his gaze chanced to fall upon a statue of the Blessed Virgin, whose superlative and incomparable beauty and grace struck him to his very heart. Falling to his knees before her and utterly infatuated, he declared: "You are truly more beautiful, more glorious and more lovely than any other creature! Therefore, I hereby renounce unconditionally all other women, and promise to love you alone!" Having thus pledged himself, he placed the ring he wore upon the finger of the image of the Queen of Heaven.

Sometime after this event, however, he was married to another woman, pursuant to normal custom and expectations. After the wedding ceremony, as he led his bride into the bridal chamber, the Blessed Virgin appeared before him, displaying the ring whereby he had once pledged himself to love her exclusively. In sad but gentle words, she reprimanded him for his infidelity to what he had promised her. He recalled his pledge and then, distressed, fell asleep, leaving his bride to herself. As he slept, Mary again appeared to him, shedding tears of chaste melancholy for the contempt which he had shown her in marrying an earthly rival.

Upon awaking and overcome by repentance for his infidelity to the Mother of God—and without any explanation or delay—the young man left his bride, his house, and his family. And he sought out the distant wilderness, where he would spend the remainder of his days in solitude and silence.

iv. THE BLESSED VIRGIN TRANSFERS ONE OF HER DEVOTEES TO A REMOTE REGION TO DO PENANCE

There was once a very rich young man who had pledged his devotion to Holy Mary, and every day prayed her Office with the greatest of ardor and sincerity. However eventually the day came for him to be married, and on that day he forgot to say his customary prayers to the glorious Mother of God.

But as he sat at the table after the wedding with his new bride and his friends and relatives, he had barely raised his hand to his mouth three times when he recalled the prayers he had neglected to say that day. Immediately he arose from the table and hastily asked the guests to excuse him for a while, and then rushed to a nearby church dedicated to the Blessed Virgin. There he said his customary prayers and devotions, and then was about to leave, to return to his wedding feast.

But the Queen of Heaven appeared before him, with downcast, melancholy eyes, as if shaded over with some heartbreaking sorrow and disappointment. The youth, struck with a feeling of guilt at his betrayal of his true Love, extended his hands and, with tears, begged for mercy from his Mistress. However blessed Mary, her voice filled with gentle reproach, said: "Depart from me, you wretched man, and go and enjoy the embraces of your new spouse, whom you have married in such cruel contempt of me!"

At these reproachful words he was overcome with regret and overwhelmed by the passion of his first love for Mary. "Far be it from me," he said, "that I should do anything contrary to your will! I am willing to sacrifice not only my wife but my very self, for the sake of your Heavenly sweetness and your perfect and incomparable beauty. Just command me and I shall do whatever you say. Just instruct me and I shall obey!" And she replied to him softly, "Follow me..."

And immediately, he was taken to a distant, unknown region, where he lived out the rest of his days in abstinence and prayer— an example to all of the most perfect chastity, silence and solitude.

'THE LITANY OF THE SEVEN KISSES'

I.   *I kiss thy hands—thy hands, whose fingers are delicate and pale as the petals of the white lotus.*

II. *I kiss thy hair, which has the luster of black jewels, and is darker than Lethe, flowering by midnight through the moonless slumber of poppy-scented lands.*

III. *I kiss thy brow, which resembles the rising moon in a valley of cedars.*

IV. *I kiss thy cheeks, where lingers a faint flush, like the reflection of a rose upheld to an urn of alabaster.*

V.   *I kiss thine eyelids, and liken them to the purple-veined flowers that close beneath the oppression of a tropic evening, in a land where the sunsets are bright as the flames of burning amber.*

VI. *I kiss thy throat, whose ardent pallor is the pallor of marble warmed by the autumn sun.*

VII.*I kiss thy mouth, which has the savor and perfume of fruits agleam with spray from a magic fountain, in the secret Paradise that we alone shall find; a Paradise whence they that come shall nevermore depart, for the waters thereof are Lethe, and the fruit is the fruit of the tree of Life.*

Clark Ashton Smith

v. THE BLESSED VIRGIN LIBERATES A SOUL DEVOTED TO HER FROM THE SENTENCE OF ETERNAL DAMNATION

There was once a certain wealthy man who had lived a life of great wickedness and sin. However, conscious of his own guilt and his need to make amends for his misdeeds, he decided to fund the construction of a monastery in honor of the Blessed Virgin, and to establish in it a community of monks once this was done. He himself resolved to become one of the monks. And so he found a suitable location and began to plan the construction. "The chapel shall go here!" he thought. "The dormitory can go there," and so forth.

Now it happened that very suddenly the man died, before his project of establishing a monastery was brought to fulfilment. And his soul was taken to its place of judgement, where angels— good and bad—stood present. The bad angels, serving as advocates of Hell's claim for the soul of the deceased, presented, as it were, the 'case for the prosecution'. Giving evidence of the man's wicked way of life, they argued very cogently that he unquestionably was thoroughly deserving of a sentence of eternal damnation.

But after about an hour one of the good angels suddenly appeared, bearing a monk's habit in his hand, and saying: "The Blessed Virgin herself sends this holy habit of monastic conversion to this man, and bestows upon him her Heavenly pardon! For, though a sinner in his life and deeds, she considers him to be one of her very own monks in his heart." Upon hearing this, the bad angels at once fled from the scene in confusion and hastened back to the fiery regions of their infernal homelands. And the soul of the man thus escaped damnation, and was granted admittance to the Kingdom of eternal bliss.

vi. AN ARMY OF DEMONS IS PUT TO FLIGHT BY THE INVOCATION OF THE HOLY NAME OF MARY

There was once a man of strong faith and charitable life, who would diligently rise each night at the hour of midnight and enter the local church alone. There he would pour out fervent prayers of gratitude and praise to the Holy Mother of God.

One night, as he set out upon his customary visit to the church, he felt himself assailed by a dense but invisible crowd of demons. Indeed, these seemed to seize upon him and hold him back forcibly, and it was only with the greatest effort that he managed to drag himself along the ground and through the door of the church. Once inside he cried out in desperation, "Hail Mary!" Immediately the stifling grasp and suffocating force of the invisible legion of fiends lightened. So again he exclaimed, "Hail Mary!", and the weight of the demonic crowd upon him again perceptibly diminished. He was now able to stand; and as he proceeded towards the altar, each time he pronounced a reverent salutation to Our Lady the force of the evil spirits was lessened, until it was dispelled completely.

vii. THE VIRGIN MARY MIRACULOUSLY CAUSES A NUN WHO WAS PLANNING ON ELOPING FROM HER CONVENT TO REMAIN FAITHFUL TO HER VOWS

There was once a wicked cleric who illicitly won the carnal affections of a young nun by means of adulation, dishonest promises and small gifts. On a certain night, this nun secretly stole the key to her convent door, so that she could leave the cloister and visit her seducer, in order to elope with him.

In the dark of the night, as she went to the entrance of the cloister to let herself out, she passed by a statue of the Blessed Virgin. Perhaps more out of habit than true devotion she bowed her head before the image and uttered, "Hail Mary," before proceeding to the locked convent door. She tried the stolen key in the lock. But as much as she tried, she could not manage to open the door. Eventually she gave up, frustrated and disappointed.

The next night she made another similar attempt. Again she saluted the image of the Mother of God in passing, and again endeavored to unlock the door. But, like the first night, she was unable to move it at all.

On the third night the nun was more anxious and desperate than before, and so did not stop to make her customary show of reverence to the image of the Blessed Mary. But this time, when she inserted the iron key into the lock, the door appeared to transform itself into the form of a human hand. This hand was now pierced and bleeding, where the nun had inserted the key into it, as if it were a nail.[3]

---

3 There is apparently a play on words here in the Latin text, with the word *clavis* ('key') resembling the word *clavus* ('nail').

A Lady of most glorious beauty and celestial radiance then appeared to the young nun, with her arm extended—she was, indeed, the possessor of this mysterious hand. And she spoke thus: "O my daughter, what are you doing? Why do you wish to pierce my hand so cruelly? A little while ago, you were saluting me reverently, and thus committing your body and soul to my maternal protection. And now, you would go forth to sin with this wicked and vile creature! Tell me—is there any mortal man at all (much less this contemptible seducer!) who is more beautiful, richer or wiser than your one true spouse, Jesus, my Son?"

Upon hearing these words the nun sincerely repented, and thereafter remained entirely committed to her vows of holy chastity.

viii. A SOLDIER, ARDENTLY DESIRING TO TAKE A CERTAIN GIRL AS HIS WIFE, IS DIVERTED FROM THIS PURPOSE BY A VISION OF THE BLESSED VIRGIN

There was once a young soldier who ardently desired to take a certain attractive girl as his wife. She, however, could by no means be induced to consent to his proposals. So the soldier went to consult the local abbot, a wise and holy man. The soldier earnestly besought that the abbot should use his influence and persuasion to encourage the girl to accept his suit, which was entirely honorable, worthy and respectable.

The abbot advised the young soldier; "My son, for the space of one year try to maintain your fleshly chastity. And each day, recite the 'Hail Mary' one hundred times, while exerting yourself in any other good works that you can. I promise that it shall bring about a good result for you!" This the soldier did with devotion and fidelity, and the time of a year quickly passed.

On the final day of that year, he knelt before the statue of Our Lady and saluted her with his customary 'Hail Mary'. But now he experienced a devotion that was strangely more profound and a desire that was more ardent than any he had ever felt before.

Then the glorious Mother of Christ suddenly appeared to him, bathed in ineffable splendor and surrounded with all the glowing radiance of Divine beauty. The soldier vaguely recalled the girl he had loved, but she now seemed as nothing to him...

The Blessed Virgin spoke to him thus, "O my friend, why do you look upon me thus, with those eyes of such longing? Do you not still desire the girl you loved?" Filled with awe, the soldier answered, "My most blessed Mistress, maiden beautiful above all others! I confess that in the past I loved foolishly. But no longer! Just permit me, I beg you, to gaze on the radiance of your face for all my days!"

Then holy Mary gently laughed at him. "My friend," she said, "you have spent the past year in prayer and good works for the sake of a desire that was merely earthly and carnal. If you now spend the next year in the same way for the sake of my Heavenly graces, I promise you that you shall be then united forever to my perfect beauty, and be dissolved in the endless bliss of the most perfect love—the love which is immortality!"

And thus the next year passed, with the soldier continuing his devotions, prayers and pious works with fidelity. As the last day of that year dawned, the soldier began suddenly to weaken in body and to lose vitality. Again, the Blessed Virgin appeared to him, even more glorious and beautiful than before. Gazing upon her, he said, "That which I have yearned for, I now behold! That which I have hoped for, I now possess." And saying this, he breathed his last....

'Caeruli Oculi'

A woman, mystic, sweet,
Whose beauty draws my soul,
Stands silent where the fleet
And singing waters roll.

Her eyes, the mirrored note
Of Heaven, merge Heaven's blue
Bestarred of lights remote,
With the sea's glaucous hue.

Within their languor set,
Smiles sadness infinite.
Tears make the sparkles wet,
And tender grows the light.

Like sea-gulls from aloft
That graze the ocean free,
Her lashes flutter soft
Upon an azure sea.

Théophile Gautier
(translated by Agnes Lee)

ix. A DEVOUT MONK IS DISCOVERED DEAD, HAVING ABOUT HIM FIVE RED ROSES INSCRIBED WITH PRAYERS

There was a certain holy monk, who each day would sing five psalms of devotion to the holy Mother of God. Now it happened one year, on the feast of St. Andrew, that all the monks gathered together for early morning prayer. The Prior, looking around, noticed that this monk—whose diligence was always exemplary—was not present amongst them. Filled with concern and surprise at his absence, the brethren, led by the Prior, hurried to the dormitory to see what was amiss.

There lay the monk in his bed, quite dead. But five roses of deepest crimson were about him—one in his mouth, two over his eyes, and two at his ears.[4] On that which was in his mouth was inscribed in golden letters the Canticle of Mary, "*My soul magnifies the Lord*". On another was the first line of the psalm, "*I called to the Lord in my tribulation*"[5]. On the next was the verse, "*O, do well unto thy faithful servant…*".[6] And on the remaining two were the verses, "*To thee I have raised my eyes…*",[7] and "*When the Lord released Zion from its captivity…*".[8]

---

4 These five crimson roses are linked with the symbolism of the five wounds of Christ. A similar symbolism is to be found in the story of Lady Benedicta of Florence, later in this volume.

5 Psalm 17.7.

6 Psalm 118.18.

7 Psalm 122.1.

8 Psalm 125.1.

All the brothers were astounded at this miracle and filled with awe and wonder. None dared to touch his body, but hastened to send for the local Archbishop. The Archbishop arrived in full dignity, with an entourage of prelates and clerics.

Approaching the body with the utmost reverence, he drew forth the crimson rose from the mouth of the deceased monk, and placed it lovingly in a vase of crystal. Indeed, there it remains to this day, the viridescence of its foliage undiminished, the rubicund hue of its flower unfaded.

And as this single red rose—the rose of love—was placed into the crystal vessel, each of the others vanished into air....

'THE SECRET ROSE'

My soul hath dreamt of a rose, whose marvelous and secret flower, fraught with an unimaginable perfume, hath never grown in any garden. Only in valleys of the shifting cloud, only among the palms and fountains of a land of mirage, only in isles beyond the seas of sunset, it blooms for a moment, and is gone.

But ever the ghost of its fragrance haunts the hall of slumber; and the women whom I meet in dreams wear always its blossom for coronal.

Clark Ashton Smith

x. THE BLESSED VIRGIN RETURNS A LOST RING TO A CERTAIN YOUTH DEVOTED TO HER, WHO THEN WEARS IT AS A PERPETUAL TOKEN OF HER LOVE

There was a man in England who, upon his deathbed, had left a precious ring to his son, saying to the youth, "Son, I want you to keep this ring carefully as long as you live, in remembrance of me." Now this youth loved and respected his father, and so obeyed him diligently. He also had a particular veneration for the Blessed Virgin Mary, and declared that he would never take a wife, since the love of the Mother of God sufficed for him.

It happened one day that, by ill fortune, the young man lost his treasured ring. Remembering his father's dying wish, he was struck with profound sorrow. His one refuge, it seemed, was prayer—and so he earnestly begged the assistance of Our Lady for him to recover the ring.

That night his sleep was troubled, and he had a dream of remarkable clarity and vividness. In this dream he was in a chapel and saw there the Blessed Virgin Mary, dazzling with celestial beauty and crowned with sidereal light. She called him to herself, and asked, "My son, what is it that you would have me do for you?"

He fell at her knees, and entreated that she restore the lost ring to his possession. Upon hearing this, she showed him her immaculate hand, upon one of the ivory-hued fingers of which was the lost ring.

Removing the ring from her finger, she lovingly placed it upon his; and, drawing near, she whispered, "Until now, you have carefully kept this ring for love of your father and respect for his memory. But henceforth, guard it even more carefully and wear it always, for love of me and my Divine Son!"

And—behold!—the next morning the man woke up to find the lost ring upon his finger, glowing with new and more resplendent radiance in the gentle light of dawn.

xi. The Blessed Virgin consoles one who is devoted to her, showing to him in a dream someone whom he later meets in waking life

There was once a soldier in France who was very devoted to the Blessed Virgin. He had heard stories of a certain girl in England who also had an equally ardent devotion to the Mother of Christ, and was inspired with a wish to meet this girl.

Now it happened one night that he had a dream in which he was in a chapel, and saw there the Virgin Mary standing before the altar and summoning him to herself. "O my son," said she, "pledge to me your loyalty, love and faithful service!" And the soldier fell to his knees, clasping Mary's hand and kissing it reverently.

Then the Blessed Virgin spoke to a certain girl who was standing by her side, "You are the witness of this act of homage, this pledge of fidelity!" The girl replied with demure humility, "Certainly, Mistress, I am."

Now it happened that, some time later, the soldier made a voyage to England. While he was there, he chanced to stay at an inn owned by the father of the same girl. When she saw the soldier she greeted him happily, as if he were an acquaintance of long standing.

The soldier, somewhat surprised at this unusual familiarity, said, "How do you know me?" She replied, "Did I not once see you pledging your loyalty to our common Mistress, our Mother Mary?" And the soldier immediately recognized the girl as the very same one he had seen in his dream, who had served as witness to his pledge of loyalty to the Queen of Heaven.

xii. The Mother of God preserves for three days the life of a thief who has been hanged, and frees him from his captors

There once was a thief who (despite his criminal profession) had a sincere devotion to the Virgin Mary. Eventually he was captured for committing a robbery, and hanged. However, the Virgin Mary, remembering the prayers and love he had towards her, preserved him from death. He thus remained suspended from the gallows for three days, unharmed and with his vitality and well-being undiminished.

Now the men who had captured and hanged him heard of this miraculous thing, and resolved instead to execute the thief by beheading him with a sword. But just as the sword was drawn and ready to strike—behold!—Our Lady appeared, and seized the sword from the hand of his would-be executioner. Stunned and bewildered, all those assembled permitted the thief, who had been visibly saved by the Mother of God herself, to go free.

The thief, however, sincerely repented of all his former crimes. He entered a monastery, where he lived out the rest of his days in penitence and prayer.

xiii. Blessed Mary, by interceding with her infant Son, saves the soul of a certain impoverished nobleman

There was once a very illustrious nobleman who, due to ill fortune and unfavorable circumstances, was reduced to the most extreme depths of poverty. In desperation, he came at last to complain against God, and to blaspheme against His Providence. Now his servant (who was thoroughly wicked) said to him, "If you follow my advice, you will soon be rich again!"

His master agreed to do so, and the servant summoned the devil himself. The devil said to the nobleman, "Deny Christ!" This, alas, the nobleman did without any hesitation or compunction. Then the devil said, "Deny the Mother of Christ!" At this point, the nobleman—despite his desperation and abandonment of the Faith—refused to do so under any circumstances. Upon hearing this unshakable refusal, the frustrated devil vanished contemptuously.

The nobleman, conscious of his great sin and blasphemy, rushed into the nearest church to beg for mercy. There, he saw a statue of the Virgin Mary holding in her arms her Son, Jesus Christ.

To his amazement, the images of both Christ and his Mother seemed to him to become animate. Mary said to her Child, "Son, please forgive this wretch for denying you. For, though he denied you, he refused to deny *me!*"

But the Divine Infant replied, "My Mother, how can I possibly forgive him, since he betrayed me without hesitation!" Mary then took the baby Jesus, and placed him upon the altar.

"Son," she said sternly, "unless you forgive him at once, I shall not take you back into my embrace!" The Savior replied, "My blessed Mother, be it done unto him according to thy word! He is forgiven everything." And immediately, with the greatest love and tenderness, the Queen of Heaven took the Infant God into her arms once more.

The impoverished noblemen, upon seeing this, was overcome by immense gratitude and overwhelming love towards both Mary and her immortal Son. That very night he departed from his home, and spent the rest of his life as a monk of the Cistercian order.

Lily of love, pure and inviolate!
Tower of ivory! Red rose of fire!
Thou hast come down our darkness to illume:
For we, close-caught in the wide nets of Fate,
Wearied with waiting for the World's Desire,
Aimlessly wandered in the House of gloom,
Aimlessly sought some slumberous anodyne
For wasted lives, for lingering wretchedness,
Till we beheld thy re-arisen shrine,
And the white glory of thy loveliness.

Oscar Wilde
from 'The New Helen'

xiv. THE BLESSED VIRGIN MIRACULOUSLY RESCUES A DISOBEDIENT MONK FROM THE ASSAULTS OF DEMONS

There was a certain man who had become a monk, yet was very negligent and undisciplined in his obedience and observance of the monastic rule. One night when all the other brethren had risen to celebrate the Office of Vigils at the appointed time, he deliberately remained resting in his bed in the dormitory.

Suddenly a host of demons appeared and beat him violently. The other monks, who were in the chapel, heard him crying out and went to see what was happening. But, though they saw him struggling and afflicted, the demons who were tormenting him were completely invisible to them. The demons, however, were put to flight by the presence of a multitude of holy monks. These then returned to continue their scheduled prayer.

The disobedient monk himself, though, refused to fulfil his duty of attending Vigils and went back to bed to sleep once more. The demons came again, and, drawing him to a distant part of the monastery, attacked him more fiercely this time.

At this, the Blessed Virgin appeared, beautiful yet strong, and said to the demons, "What are you doing to this poor monk?!"

The demons replied, "He is disobedient to the Holy Rule of his vocation; he is not following the monastic timetable properly. He thoroughly deserves this treatment!"

To this the Queen of Angels replied, "Perhaps that is true. But you are employed as ministers of hell, not as police officers for Heaven! It is not *your* responsibility to take vengeance on behalf of the Lord." Having said this, the demons departed, with grumbling acknowledgment of the truth of what the Mother of Mercy had said.

xv. A SIMPLE BUT DEVOUT MAIDEN GLOWS WITH A WONDROUS LUMINESCENCE WHENEVER SHE SAYS THE 'HAIL MARY'

In a city somewhere in the Kingdom of Hungary there was a young maiden who was somewhat simple of mind, yet very devoted to God and his most glorious Mother. She knew no prayer except for the first half of the 'Hail Mary'; that is to say, "Hail Mary, full of grace, the Lord is with thee." But she said this verse constantly, without intermission. And as she did so, a glowing luminescence, like the light of a small sun, would always appear above her head.

The local bishop heard about this, and being a holy and generous man, carefully and patiently taught this simple maiden the other part of the prayer, namely; "Blessed art thou amongst women, and blessed is the fruit of thy womb, Jesus."[9]

But then, when the girl began to recite the complete prayer, the glowing radiance which had formerly emanated from her was now seen no more. Upon learning this, the bishop was distressed and prayed to the Lord about it. And the Lord answered him, in a kind yet firm voice, "Where Divine grace abounds, human instruction is unnecessary!"

The bishop then visited the girl, and implored her to return to her former practice of saying only the first half of the prayer,

---

9 It is to be noted that at this time the *Ave Maria* or Angelic Salutation consisted only of the first half of the modern version of the 'Hail Mary', i.e. the part preceding "Holy Mary, Mother of God ...". Thus when the bishop teaches the girl the remainder of the prayer, it extends only to the first half of the modern 'Hail Mary'.

"Hail Mary, full of grace, the Lord is with thee." This she did, and the resplendent light which had formerly surrounded her began once more to shine.

xvi. The Virgin Mary deters a monk from his intention of committing theft and leaving his monastery

There was once a certain poor and desperate scholar. Though he had been gifted with keen intelligence and had worked hard to acquire a basic literary education, he had no professional prospects or opportunities for advancement in the world. So, for the sake of committing a large-scale theft and thereby making himself wealthy, he became a monk at a nearby monastery. Each day he would consider the best way of fulfilling his evil plan. But a whole year elapsed and he found no suitable opportunity for stealing anything of substantial value, and so he resolved to leave the monastery and try his chances elsewhere.

But just as he was about to leave he heard the bell ring, indicating that Mass was about to begin. For reasons which he did not fully grasp, he hesitated in his plan to depart, and thought to himself, "It will be best if I wait until winter is over." Thus he went to the church according to the usual monastic practice, and from then on continued to live as a monk.

Now for the next twenty years, he continued in his plans to leave the monastery. But for various reasons, he never actually did. And eventually he was ordained as a priest.

Once ordained to the sacred ministry of the Church, however, he saw that his prospects of life outside the monastery had greatly improved. He then determined with greater resolution than before to depart from the community at his next opportunity.

But that night he had a dream. He was celebrating the holy Eucharist at an altar at which there was an image of the Blessed

Virgin holding Christ in her arms. As he elevated the consecrated host, the Divine Infant snatched it from his hands. Struck at his heart by this, the monk implored Christ with tears that he should return the precious Sacrament to him. And he promised that if Christ did return it to him, thereafter he should never consider violating his vows and leaving the cloister. And indeed, upon hearing this, the Child-God returned the sacred host to his wavering priest.

The next morning, the monk openly confessed all that had happened throughout his life to the whole assembly of brethren—his initial joining of the monastery in order to commit theft, his long-enduring plans to break his vows and leave the community, and the vision which had come to him in his dream on the previous night. Shortly after, the abbot of the monastery died, and this monk—now an old man—was himself unanimously elected abbot.

xvii. The Blessed Virgin reprimands a certain dissipated soldier, and at last draws him to Heaven

There was once a very dissipated and dishonest soldier, who nevertheless would prayerfully salute Blessed Mary with great frequency and devotion. One day he was in a chapel dedicated to the Virgin, and reciting his customary daily prayers in her honor.

Now suddenly a great sensation of hunger came upon him, to the point where he felt so ravenous he could almost eat his own hands. At this moment, a woman appeared before him of miraculous beauty surrounded with refulgent splendor. She bore in her hand a dish filled with wonderful food, which she offered to the soldier. However, the dish itself was utterly squalid, and encrusted with the most revolting filth. So despite his hunger and the quality of the food, the soldier declined to accept what was offered him.

The woman said to him, "Do you know who I am?" The soldier replied that he did not. "I am the Mother of God!" said she. "Why is it, my son, that you do not accept the food which is offered you?"

The soldier became somewhat embarrassed at his own refusal, but nevertheless replied honestly. "My Lady," said he, "it is because of the filth covering the dish that I find myself unwilling to take this food."

The Blessed Virgin looked at him intently, her eyes alight with celestial wisdom. "And similarly," she declared, "I do not find the dish of prayers which you offer me daily to be palatable or acceptable, since you serve them in a vessel which is begrimed with filth—that is to say, your wicked mode of life. But if you undertake to cleanse the vessel of your life by conversion and repentance, then, my son, I shall be delighted to accept the prayers and service you offer me!" Having said this, she disappeared from his sight.

Thereafter the soldier sought out a deserted place and lived the rest of his life—some thirty years—as a hermit. And as he lay upon his death bed, the glorious Queen of Heaven appeared to him once more, and led his soul, now cleansed of its former sin, to the celestial Kingdom of Paradise.

xviii. Our Lady rescues a young boy who had almost drowned from the waters of a rapid river

There was a certain family which had in their house a statue of the Blessed Virgin. Both the father and mother of this family would reverently salute the statue whenever they passed by. They had a young son who, without fully understanding what he was doing, adopted the same practice of saluting the image. When he asked his mother whom it was that the statue depicted, she replied simply, "It is Our Lady." For this reason, the boy assumed that she was merely an important noblewoman of the district.

One day the boy was walking on the banks of the local river, which was flowing very rapidly at the time. Suddenly the waters swept up, and washed the boy into the turbulent stream. Some onlookers rushed to tell the boy's mother, who then hurried to the bank. She stood calling out to her son, but saw his body—apparently almost dead—being tossed and turned violently by the waves.

But then the body was, as if by an invisible hand, drawn up onto a small island in the center of the stream, and the boy regained consciousness. His mother spoke to him, "My son! Tell me, what has happened?"

The boy replied, "A lady has drawn me from the waters." But none understood who 'the lady' was to whom he referred.

But when they arrived at home, the boy saw the statue of the Blessed Virgin. Pointing at it, with the greatest simplicity he declared, "*There* is the Lady who drew me from the waters!"

xix. A MAN UNKNOWINGLY DEFENDS HIMSELF AGAINST THE DEVIL BY MEANS OF SAYING A SINGLE 'HAIL MARY' EVERY MORNING AND EVERY EVENING

There was a certain soldier who had a servant who had worked for him for many years. But unknown to the man, this servant was actually the devil, concealing himself beneath a disguise. The man trusted his 'old servant', and often acted upon his advice. He therefore frequently did imprudent and unwise things. But somehow, despite the old servant's wicked advice, he never actually fell into a state of mortal sin, or lost the grace of God and communion with the Church.

Now a certain holy man perceived that this servant was, in fact, the devil in disguise. And he said to him, "How is it that you have been the close companion and advisor of this soldier for so many years, and yet you have not once succeeded in corrupting him or drawing him away from God?"

The devil, in frustration, replied to the saint; "Every morning and every evening this man says just one 'Hail Mary'. The one he says in the morning protects his soul throughout the day, and the one he says at evening keeps him safe at night. Thus I can never overcome him!"

Having said this, the devil departed; and the 'old servant' was never seen again…

Uncharmable charmer
Of Bacchus and Mars,
In the sounding rebounding
Abyss of the stars!
O Virgin in armour,
Thine arrows unsling
In the brilliant resilient,
First rays of the spring!

By the force of the fashion
Of love, when I broke
Through the shroud, through the cloud,
Through the storm, through the smoke,
To the mountain of passion
Volcanic, that woke ---
By the rage of the mage
I invoke, I invoke!

[...]

You were mine, O my Saint,
My maiden, my mate,
By the might of the right
Of the night of our fate.
Though I fall, though I faint,
Though I char, though I choke,
By the hour of our power,
I invoke, I invoke!

Aleister Crowley
from 'Pan to Artemis'

NOBLE DAUGHTERS OF MARY

BY **IPPOLITO MARRACCI**

i. Princess Ada of Avesnes

Princess Ada of Avesnes[10] revered the glorious Mother of God with the greatest devotion of heart. Among her works of piety towards the Virgin Queen, each day she recited the 'Hail Mary' sixty times—twenty times lying prostrate on the ground, twenty times kneeling, and twenty times standing, either in her chapel or in her bedroom or in some other secret place she chose.

There was a secluded and unfrequented forest called Broqeuroy near Princess Ada's castle, in which a certain holy hermit lived a life of prayer and solitude. Once he saw a strange vision (as the hermit himself relates), in the middle of the day when he was fully awake. In this waking vision, blessed Mary appeared to him. The Mother of God sat upon a wonderful throne, with two saints—St. Waldetrude and St. Aldegonde— lying at her feet in supplication. They were complaining bitterly to her about the actions of Ada's husband, the Prince Theodore, who had foolishly burnt down churches dedicated to them.[11] They earnestly requested of Mary that she should take revenge upon the prince for his impiety.

When these two saints continued to complain long and insistently, the Blessed Virgin responded to them, "I beg you,

---

10 A town in northern France.

11 According to the twelfth-century *Liber de Restauratione Abbatiae Sancti Martini Tornacensis* of Herman of Tournai (which seems to be the original source of this narration), Theodore had burnt down convents dedicated to St. Waldetrude and St. Aldegonde in a war with a certain neighboring nobleman.

please desist from your demands! At present I do not wish to punish Prince Theodore, although he admittedly has done this very foolish thing. For his wife is none other than Princess Ada, and she offers to me every day her faithful and loving service, and through this has become my very dear friend. For this reason, I cannot bear the thought of any misfortune or affliction befalling either her or her husband!"

Upon hearing this, the saints were perplexed. They asked the Queen of Heaven what was the service which Ada offered to her. Mary replied, "Every day she prays the 'Hail Mary'. To hear this prayer, which echoes the salutation which the archangel Gabriel spoke to me, brings me more delight than any other earthly thing! And Princess Ada recites this prayer unfailingly, no less than sixty times each day. She says it twenty times while lying down upon the ground, twenty times while kneeling and twenty times while standing erect, either in her chapel or her bedroom or in some secret place in solitude"

But the two disgruntled saints, Waldetrude and Aldegonde, would not be deterred so easily from their complaining, but continued to insist that the Blessed Virgin should take punitive action on their behalf for the churches which Theodore had burnt down. To silence them, Mary said, "All I ask is that you allow me to wait for a while before attending to this matter. When the appropriate time comes, I promise that I shall administer justice just as is deserved, but in such a way that Princess Ada should not suffer the distress of being permanently separated from her beloved husband."

Now, Theodore and Ada, though they had been married for a long time, had never had any children. Theodore's relatives were greatly perturbed by this fact, as it meant that there would be no heir to his princely estates and title. Accordingly, they resolved to seek to have the marriage dissolved, in order that Theodore might be able to take a new wife who would bear him offspring.

So they went to the local prelate, Odo, the bishop of Cambria, who was also Abbot of the Abbey of St. Martin in Tournai.[12] They advised him that their kinsmen, Prince Theodore, was, in fact, related distantly by blood to his wife, Princess Ada, and that the marriage should therefore be declared to be invalid.

Bishop Odo investigated the matter, and found that it was quite true—for Theodore and Ada were, indeed, distantly related by blood. Therefore, acting in accordance with the strict requirements of canon law, he declared their marriage to be invalid. So the couple, despite having lived as man and wife for more than twenty years, were separated and—in humble obedience to the ruling of the holy Church—considered themselves no longer to be married.

Less than half a year had elapsed since this separation and annulment, when Theodore happened to be hunting alone in the woods. A certain enemy of his, a violent and cunning man by the name of Isaac of Barlemont, knew him to be hunting without companions and guards, and so waited in hiding in ambush for him. Taking him by surprise, he slew Prince Theodore, leaving him dead. In due course, his body was found and taken to the nearby monastery at Liessies, where he was buried in the church next to the presidential chair of the abbot.[13] This monastery had, in fact, been established and funded by Theodore and Ada some years previously.

Princess Ada had now apparently lost her husband in a double sense. For firstly, her marriage to Theodore had been declared invalid; and, secondly, his earthly life had been brought to a premature and violent end. Seeking refuge and consolation in the Lord and renouncing henceforth all worldly splendor

---

12 This bishop, Blessed Odo of Cambria, was the author of several books on theological subjects.

13 This abbey church survives to this day.

and luxury, she betook herself to the monastery which she had founded with Theodore, and in which his mortal remains now rested. She had constructed for herself there a stone tower adjoining the monastery church, and so, in truth, was never really separated from Prince Theodore. Thus, just as Mary had promised the two saints, Prince Theodore was duly punished for his unfortunate acts of impiety, but Ada was never permanently separated from him.

In the peaceful refuge of her tower, the Princess lived out her days in prayer and solitude. And she never ceased to offer her service to our blessed Lady, by reciting the 'Hail Mary' sixty times a day—twenty times lying prostrate on the ground, twenty times kneeling, and twenty times standing.

Since Theodore and Ada had begotten no children, in due course their castle, lands and noble titles passed to the prince's nephew, Gosceguinus. Gosceguinus heard the story of his aunt's wonderful piety towards the great Mother of God. Inspired by her example, he himself took up the practice of saying the 'Hail Mary' sixty times each day, and required each of his soldiers and servants to do the same. Now Gosceguinus, despite his devotion to Our Lady, did many wicked things during his life; but thanks to Mary's merciful and indulgent intercession, he came at last to a good and holy end. For, towards the end of his life when he was afflicted by a grave illness, he entered the same monastery which his uncle Theodore had constructed, and became a monk there. He finished his life in prayer and penitence, and was buried next to his uncle in the monastery church.

Princess Ada herself passed away peacefully in her tower beside the church in about the year 1100.

'HYMN'

At morn—at noon—at twilight dim—
Maria! thou hast heard my hymn!
In joy and wo—in good and ill—
Mother of God, be with me still!
When the Hours flew brightly by,
And not a cloud obscured the sky,
My soul, lest it should truant be,
Thy grace did guide to thine and thee;
Now, when storms of Fate o'ercast
Darkly my Present and my Past,
Let my Future radiant shine
With sweet hopes of thee and thine!

Edgar Allan Poe

ii. Princess Angela of Bohemia

Princess Angela, the daughter of Vladislav the King of Bohemia,[14] was born in Prague, the capital city of her father's kingdom. From her earliest years, she was committed to a convent of nuns to receive her education. One evening, when she was saying her prayers in the chapel, she prostrated herself before the high altar in adoration. And it happened that she fell into a gentle slumber, and saw in a vision the glorious Mother of God appear. Blessed Mary was surrounded by a radiant choir of angels, who sang her praises in soaring, celestial harmonies.

She suddenly woke up, but the vision did not immediately disappear. For she continued to hear the angelic voices singing thus:

> Hail, O Queen enthroned above,
> Whom we angels serve with love,
> Brightest star of Heaven's height,
> Mirror of God's holy light![15]

Once this enchanting hymn of praise had reached its conclusion, she heard a voice—loving and sweet, yet full of power—instructing her to take flight from where she was, and to undertake a pilgrimage to the holy city of Jerusalem. There, the voice told her, she was to become a nun, taking the habit of the Order of Our Lady of Mount Carmel.

---

14 That is, King Vladislav II.

15 Some liberty has been taking in translating these verses, to emulate the rhyme of the original.

But meanwhile Angela's father, the King of Bohemia, decided that it was time for his daughter to be married. So he called her from the convent where she was studying back to the palace. Now, a prince from Hungary, the son of the king of that nation and heir to its throne, was visiting Prague at the time. He was a man of remarkably handsome appearance, and was himself captivated by Angela's beauty. So he requested her hand in marriage from her father the king. As far as her family was concerned, it would have been in every respect an ideal alliance.

Yet Angela was determined to retain her virginity and to follow her vocation to consecrated life. So one night, on the instructions of an angel, she secretly fled from the palace. She left a note, written by her own hand in Latin, which told them about her visions and her intention to become a nun. At the end of this note, she added the words of Christ, "You shall seek me, but you shall not find me!"[16]

She set out upon her journey, disguising herself by exchanging her fine attire for the garment of a man. After travelling for a whole day and passing through a great place of solitude, she found a small farmhouse, inhabited by a family who kindly offered her shelter. Now, as it happened this family were not Catholics, but had been led astray by the deceptions of schismatics. Angela, filled with compassion for them and zeal for the Gospel, expounded the truths and mysteries of the Catholic Church, and offered prayers commending them to the guidance of God and the Blessed Virgin.

Then she continued her solitary pilgrimage with determination. Often it came to pass that, exhausted by a long day's travel, she would find some well-sheltered and comfortable site, ideal for her to take her rest. Once when this had occurred, and the morning light aroused her from slumber, she beheld a

---

16 John 7.34.

vision of the glorious Mother of God. And blessed Mary declared to her that it was she herself who prepared for Angela suitable places to take her nightly rest.

After a lengthy and arduous journey, Angela eventually arrived in the holy city of Jerusalem. She exchanged the male disguise which she had been wearing throughout her pilgrimage for female dress, and visited all the holy places in the city, her heart filled with indescribable love and wonder. Once she had done this, she found the convent of the Carmelite nuns there. And, just as she had been instructed by the Blessed Virgin, she besought admission to the community and became a nun.

The years passed by and she lived a life of piety, simplicity, humility, and obedience. But one Saturday—a day which she dedicated to the Queen of Heaven with the greatest devotion— an angel appeared before her, robed in golden light. The angel spoke to her of many marvelous things, revealing the hidden treasures of the divine mysteries and the glories of Heaven. He also gave her a most serious warning, counselling her thus, "My daughter, you must flee from here with all haste! For God, on account of the sins and crimes of the Christian people in this region, has resolved to permit the infidels to conquer this city and take possession of it for a period of time. Return to your native land, and pray for your own people. For, truly, a great calamity is to befall them too!"

Obeying this counsel, Princess Angela returned to her father's royal palace at Prague. She was indefatigable in proclaiming the warning which she had received from the angel of the coming of divine wrath upon the kingdom. Indeed, this dire prophecy was fulfilled by the outbreak of heresy and schism, which took hold of Bohemia from 1410 and continues to rage there till this present day.[17]

---

17 That is, when the author was writing in 1659.

Angela also received many other visions and divine revelations, which she committed to writing. These included a heavenly revelation concerning the Immaculate Conception of the Blessed Virgin. The details of this revelation on the Immaculate Conception are described by Bartholomew Guerrero in his book *De Conceptione Beata,* by Sebastian de Novaes in his *De Lilio inter Spinas,* and in the *Armamentarium Seraphicum* edited by Pedro de Alva y Astorga,[18] as well as by many other learned authors.

Princess Angela of Bohemia died around the year 1230. She gave forth her immortal spirit into the embrace of her beloved spouse, Jesus Christ, on the sixth day of July.[19] The story of her life has been written in a most elegant style by Fr. Joannes Paulus a Porta[20] of our own congregation.[21]

---

18 The full names of these authors have been added by the translator. *De Lilio inter Spinas* was published in 1648, and the *Armamentarium Seraphicum* (a compilation of texts and extracts concerning the Immaculate Conception of Mary) was published in 1649. It has not been possible to locate a copy of Guerrero's work, nor to ascertain its date of publication.

19 Blessed Angela of Bohemia died in 1243. Apparently, Marracci did not have access to this information, hence his providing 1230 as the approximate time of her passing. Although she was never formally canonized, she is often referred to as 'St. Angela' and is included with that designation in the *Acta Sanctorum,* in which her feast day is given as July 6.

20 This work was unpublished at the time of Marracci's writing, but existed in manuscript form. It apparently remains unpublished to this day.

21 That is, the Order of Clerics Regular of the Mother of God.

iii. Lady Alexandra of Aragon

In the Kingdom of Aragon, one of the wealthiest and most illustrious noble families had a single daughter, Alexandra. She was of remarkable beauty and very strong faith, and, while still a youth, enrolled herself in a pious society or sisterhood dedicated to the Blessed Virgin Mary. Her membership of this committed her to the praying of the Rosary and other Marian devotions each day. Nevertheless, Lady Alexandra, like many other young people, became distracted by various worldly vanities. Not infrequently she would neglect her promised devotions to the Mother of God, in order to concern herself with matters of dress and jewelry and the cultivation of her outward appearance. Alas, the temptations and distractions of this passing world are very difficult to avoid, especially for those graced with wealth, beauty, and high status!

But it was Alexandra's beautiful appearance which brought her to a tragic end. For two young noblemen became infatuated with her, and their rivalry was as bitter as their feelings were passionate and amorous. It was not long before this rivalry boiled over into open violence. They fought a furious duel, which resulted in the death of both of them.

Naturally, Alexandra was deeply shocked and disturbed by this. She had done nothing to encourage either of the young men in their affections, yet she very sincerely regretted their deaths. But a relative of one of the young men who had died secretly blamed Alexandra for his kinsman's premature death. Maddened with wrath and sorrow, he swore himself to revenge against the noble maiden, innocent though she was. So one night he stealthily crept into the palace in which Alexandra lived. And—dreadful as it is to say—while she slept, he cut off her head with the sharp blade of his dagger!

This head he took with him for some distance, until he disposed of it by casting it into a deep well. The horror and grief of her family may readily be imagined to discover the death of their beloved Alexandra. The fact that she had suffered violence and that her whole body could not be interred with due reverence further augmented their pain.

But after five months had elapsed, the great St. Dominic was travelling through the area. He received a vision of the Blessed Virgin, who told him that the mortal remains of one of her most devoted daughters lay in the depths of a particular well. So the illustrious saint went there; and, lo, the head of Lady Alexandra immediately arose up from the well! And not only did it rise up for the place where it had so long been concealed, but it was filled with vitality and animation.

Floating in the air, it spoke to St. Dominic, saying, "Holy Father, I earnestly wish to make my confession to you!" Dominic, though astonished at what he beheld, naturally acquiesced to this humble and pious request. He duly heard Alexandra's confession, especially of her omission of some of her promised daily devotions to the Queen of Heaven. Moreover, the Blessed Sacrament of the Body and Blood of Christ was given to her re-animated head. And the head of Alexandra continued to live and to converse with St. Dominic for some two days. After this, it vanished from sight once more.

But about fifteen days later, the deceased maiden's head appeared to St. Dominic again. This time it was radiant and joyful, and glowed with all the brilliance of a small star. Alexandra, through this vision, related to Dominic how, until now, she had been suffering in Purgatory, and undergoing the necessary recompense for her various sins and failings. And she implored the saint to warn the members of the pious society in which she had been enrolled not to neglect the daily devotions to which they had committed themselves, lest they too should experience the pains of Purgatory.

"But," she concluded happily, "such torments are now finished for me, through the mercy of God and the power of the sacraments. In the company of all the saints, I share the infinite joy of the angels and exult with the Queen of Heaven in the glorious vision of the Most Holy Trinity!"

Lady Alexandra of Aragon died around the year of Our Lord 1218. And though her death was violent, we may be confident that she now enjoys ineffable and eternal peace.

iv. Lady Benedicta of Florence

There was a certain noble woman called Lady Benedicta who resided in the city of Florence, during the era when the great St. Dominic lived. Although her name, Benedicta, means 'a woman who is blessed', her own actions and mode of life were far removed from this high appellation. For she was begotten of adulterous parents, and, without any example of moral rectitude, she grew up surrounded by licentious behavior, debauched feasting and every kind of laxity and vice. Little by little she herself sank into the mire of sin and immorality. Unfortunate circumstances and bad influences eventually led her to employment as a kind of high-class courtesan. Despite the affluence and distinction of the circles in which she moved, her life was essentially the same as that of a worker in a brothel—something which is surely the nadir of shame and disgrace for every good woman.

Now in those days, St. Dominic was energetically engaged in his great missions of preaching the Gospel. This he confined not to one city only, but traversed the whole expanse of Italy. Lady Benedicta heard of the fame of this wondrous and ardent preacher from her clients and friends, and was naturally curious to see and hear him to learn what it was that had inspired such profound and widespread admiration. So she betook herself to listen to him when he visited Florence.

As she listened to him, along with a large crowd, the words of his fervent preaching sunk deep into the heart and soul of this noble but licentious courtesan. She was overcome with compunction and tears of repentance. As Dominic was about to leave, she fell on her knees and made a full confession to him of her many sins. The saint listened attentively, gazing upon her without severity but with eyes filled with compassion and mercy. Indeed, there was nothing which gave him greater joy than to win the soul of one of his brothers or sisters back to salvation and the blessed flock of God's Catholic Church.

Dominic spoke to Benedicta, and said, "My daughter, I hear you and reprehend you for your many sins. And though these sins are without number, I absolve you of them all!" He also urged her with sincere charity and kindly fervor that henceforth she should vow herself to chastity, choosing as her Spouse none other than the Lord Jesus Christ.

Benedicta at once adopted a life of conversion and sanctity. She chose the Blessed Virgin, the immaculate exemplar and paradigm of all virtues, as her special patroness. Fortified and protected by a life of strict austerity, she fought hard to preserve perfect chastity, not only in her body but in her heart and mind as well. She protected and cultivated her new-found virtues zealously, and sought to expel from her soul whatever remained of the venom of her former lasciviousness.

But her path to full repentance and conversion was not easy, for a wicked demon soon began to torment her. God permitted this to continue for one year. During that time, St. Dominic interceded with the Lord on Benedicta's behalf, and in the end she was freed from the affliction and anxiety which the demon had caused her.

The same blessed saint, Dominic, the father and founder of the noble Order of Preachers, instructed Benedicta in her life of prayer and devotion, lest she should fall into error or lose heart. Amongst his other counsels, he advised her to say the Rosary, consisting of fifty repetitions of the 'Hail Mary', with five repetitions of the 'Our Father' interspersed among them. This prayer, he taught her, was a most efficacious and powerful remedy for temptation and despair. Also, he advised Benedicta that the frequent invocation of the names of Jesus and Mary was a sure means of cleansing the soul from all the stains and pollution which it had acquired through her earlier manner of living.

After receiving such sound and salubrious guidance from the wise St. Dominic, Benedicta succeeded in living a life of piety, devotion and virtue for some time. But—alas!—after a while she fell again into the foul swamp of vice from which she had managed to arise. Indeed, this time her debauchery and sin was even worse than before. Just as a river, when it has been damned up for a period, will suddenly rush on with greater rapidity and turbulence than previously, so did Benedicta now rush headlong into the depths of sins. Casting off the restraints she had imposed upon herself during her time of virtue and chastity, she now plunged into the sins of the flesh with renewed avidity and desire.

When news of this came to the ears of blessed Dominic, he was horrified. He grieved deeply for her, and also for the many men whose hearts and souls Benedicta's beauty and voluptuousness had captured and led into corruption and even death. So he came to the palace of Lady Benedicta, and forced his way in. With zealous animation and indignation, he drove forth from her abode all who had gathered there to indulge in vile debauchery with her, compelling them to leave her dwelling like a herd of filthy pigs.

He took Benedicta and led her to the nearest church, where he heard her confession. She cried bitterly and sincerely, and she was filled with guilt and shame for her lapse back into her former sins. The abundance of her tears testified to the acuteness of her compunction, and revealed that her true self—the woman within—still aspired to a life of virtue and purity. Dominic exhorted her to resume her praying of the Rosary with diligence, and to remain vigilant in the observance of Christian virtue. Whenever she felt the demon of temptation to be attacking her, she was to use the two sacred names of Jesus and Mary as invincible weapons against him, for truly the sweet sound of these holy names cannot be endured by any demonic entity. Benedicta followed these instructions assiduously, and, in the fervor of her conversion, became like a second St. Thaïs.[22]

A little while after this, she received a vision in which she was taken up before the tribunal of judgement of God, who is the incorruptible Judge of both the living and the dead. She saw the book of her life brought forth and opened, revealing her innumerable sins inscribed therein. She also saw in her vision the dreadful punishment and torments which her sins had justly merited. Moreover, a multitude of hellish fiends and monsters appeared before her, eager to seize upon her soul and drag it away to the infernal regions of endless pain. When she beheld all of these fearsome and horrendous sights, she cried out, "Woe to my parents, whose dissolute negligence first plunged me into this deep ocean of vice! Woe to all of those who flattered me when I was a mere girl, and showered me with gifts and trinkets in order to corrupt my virtue!" And she wept bitterly.

Yet, through her tears, she perceived St. Dominic appearing suddenly before the tribunal. He spoke up on her behalf, and told of how Benedicta had humbly prayed many times upon her knees before the Virgin Mother of God, and how she had implored the protection and help of holy Mary with sighs and weeping. Dominic interceded for her with tears and lamentations of his own, and the Mother of God herself appeared and joined in with his intercessions before the awesome tribunal of Divine Judgement. They earnestly pleaded that Benedicta be granted further time to obtain forgiveness for her sins.

---

22 St. Thaïs was a wealthy and famous courtesan in fourth century Roman Egypt. She was converted by St. Paphnutias, and thereafter followed a life of strict austerity, solitude, and penitence. Various versions of the story of her life were widely circulated through the Middle Ages.

With such powerful advocates, this grace was granted to her by God, the omnipotent and all-merciful Judge. And she saw that all the sins and misdeeds which were recorded in the book of her life had been erased, so that the pages of the book of her life were clean, radiant and pure!

As she marveled at these things in grateful wonder, suddenly she was drawn up in rapture, and the glorious Queen of Heaven stood before her. With her own immaculate hand, she gave to Lady Benedicta five roses of deepest, glowing crimson.[23]

Upon the first of these roses was written in letters of gold, "Be mindful always both of your sins and of the divine mercy which has overcome them!"

On the second rose was similarly inscribed, "Remember the most bitter passion and death of our Lord Jesus Christ, by which the foulness and depravity of your past sins is revealed, for these could be washed away by nothing else but the precious blood of the most innocent Son of God!"

The third rose bore the message, "Recall poor Adam, and the wretched progeny of Adam! For a single sin he was deprived of the joys of paradise. By that one fault, he was exiled from the blissful garden of Eden, and earned for all his descendants a sentence of sorrow and toil. And think of all those who have sinned and have thereby come to know grave punishments and afflictions. And, in contemplating this, recall that your own sins far exceeded those of Adam and of many of those damned to eternal torments. And yet *you* have been mercifully freed from any debt of punishment."

---

23 Five red roses (and similar images) were often understood as symbols or reminders of the five wounds of Christ, as in Chapter IX of the collection of St. Celestine. A comparison may be made with the five arrows placed in the heart of Blessed Dorothea of Prussia (in a later chapter of this work).

On the fourth of the roses, Benedicta read written in gold: "Be mindful of the singular benefits Heaven has bestowed upon you. In the first place, you were born and raised in a pious land and so you were imbued with the true faith. Do not forget how many lands and nations and peoples do not have this tremendous privilege; for the majority of the world's population live and die without knowing the reality of the spiritual realm, yet you—although unworthy—have received the illumination of the light of divine truth. And what is more, you were called back from the way of perdition to the way of life, and your own sins were made manifest to you. Recognize this multitude of gifts of the most merciful Lord freely given to you—including life, religion and conversion—and see His celestial generosity, which surpasses that of any other!"

The fifth of the roses also bore a message, inscribed upon its petals and leaves as if written on a sheet of paper. It read thus: "Do not forget the grave punishments and afflictions by which Divine Justice always punishes wrongdoers, both in this life and the eternal hereafter! Think of what befell Cain, who murdered his brother Abel; or what happened to Shem, who mocked his father Noah. Keep in mind the thousands of common criminals, who are hanged to death simply for a small act of theft. Yet your own sins and iniquities are far graver and far more numerous; and yet the supreme Judge has imposed upon you no such punishment. Consider how many, who for lighter errors than those of which you have been guilty, have incurred the everlasting torments of eternal damnation. Such souls would rather be granted the smallest opportunity of repenting for their sins than possession of all the treasures of the earth! But to you has been granted an abundance of time, which has been denied to them, and in this time you still have the opportunity of correcting your life and escaping the dreadful punishment that must otherwise await."

Following this vision, Benedicta contemplated deeply what she had witnessed. She remembered always the messages inscribed in gold upon the five roses given to her by the Blessed Virgin, keeping them like precious treasures and healing remedies in her heart. The mode of life which she thenceforth adopted moved all to admiration. For she exhorted many of her fellow citizens of Florence to adopt the practice of praying the Marian Rosary, which is such an effective and powerful medicine for all ailments of the soul.

Some time later, Benedicta received another remarkable vision. In this vision, Christ appeared before her holding the same book of her life which she had previously seen. "Behold!" said the Savior, "This is the book of your life. Formerly, it was black and horrendous with the list of your numberless sins, but now it has been rendered radiant and white. For your own tears of penitence and the five splendid roses which my glorious Mother gave to you have cleansed it, and transformed its murky darkness into the pure whiteness of Heaven's snow. It behooves you now, my beloved daughter, to write a fresh story upon its clean and unstained pages. Write therein a tale of purity of life. Inscribe all the wonders of patience, love and devotion. And let its pages continue long and happily—yea, even unto eternal life!"

After this vision, the Mother of God again appeared to Lady Benedicta. She assured her that whatever her divine Son had asked of her she would most certainly be able to accomplish and fulfill, with the assistance and support of the holy Rosary.

Lady Benedicta of Florence died peacefully and in a state of grace around the year of Our Lord 1220.

Madonna, mistress. I would build for thee
An altar deep in the sad soul of me;
And in the darkest corner of my heart,
From mortal hopes and mocking eyes apart,
Carve of enamelled blue and gold a shrine
For thee to stand erect in, Image divine!
And with a mighty Crown thou shalt be crowned
Wrought of the gold of my smooth Verse, set round
With starry crystal rhymes; and I will make,
O mortal maid, a Mantle for thy sake,
And weave it of my jealousy, a gown
Heavy, barbaric, stiff, and weighted down
With my distrust, and broider round the hem
Not pearls, but all my tears in place of them.
[...]
While all the love and worship in my sense
Will be sweet smoke of myrrh and frankincense.
Ceaselessly up to thee, white peak of snow,
My stormy spirit will in vapours go!

Charles Baudelaire
from 'To a Madonna'
(translated by Frank Pearce Sturm)

v. Queen Blanche of France

Queen Blanche was the wife of King Louis VIII of France, who was a pious and devout monarch.[24] And she was the mother of King Louis IX, who gained the glory of sainthood and was arguably the most holy monarch which Heaven's sun has ever beheld.[25] Foremost in her life of faith and prayer, Blanche had a singular devotion to the most glorious Empress of the Angels, Mary, the Mother of God.

It transpired that Blanche and Louis had lived as man and wife for many years, but had not begotten any children. Indeed, this was a source of considerable anxiety and disappointment to both of them. Now in those days, St. Dominic, the founder of the Order of Preachers, was travelling through France, preaching the Gospel and attending to matters related to the Dominican friars. The queen heard of his reputation for sanctity and humbly approached him, requesting his intercession that she and her husband might be blessed by God with children.

Dominic listened to her with compassion, and told her that if she truly wanted to conceive a child, she should pray the holy Rosary with great ardor and intention. Moreover, he counselled Blanche that she should encourage as many others as she possibly could to adopt the practice of saying this same prayer. The saint

---

24 Louis VIII was twelve years of age at the time of this marriage, and Blanche (who was the third daughter of King Alfonso VIII of Castile) was only a year older. The marriage was not consummated until several years afterwards.

25 King Louis IX is the only King of France to have been formally declared a saint. He was canonized in 1297.

told her that whoever said this prayer in honor of the Mother of God was assured of being favorably heard by God himself.

Once Queen Blanche had learnt how to say the Rosary from St. Dominic, she not only said it every day with the greatest fidelity, but she herself proceeded to teach it to others with unflagging enthusiasm. She took diligent care that it should be promoted throughout the entire Kingdom of France.

As for her prayer for herself and her husband that she should bear children, it was very soon answered once she had taken up the daily recitation of the Rosary. For she conceived a son, who would go on to become King Louis IX. This pious king became a radiant example of sanctity, whose holiness was confirmed by the vast number of miracles and wonders which he performed and experienced. Very deservedly was he enrolled by the Church amongst the canon of the saints.

If any should be inclined to doubt the devotion of Blanche to the holy Rosary, they should consider the Royal Abbey of the Blessed Mary close to Pontoise, which was founded by this devout queen. The charter by which she established this abbey still survives, and in it one may read the following lines:

> Motivated by our desire to set up a true house of the Lord, which should contribute to the honor of God and especially to that of his glorious ever-Virgin Mother, we hereby establish this monastery as an Abbey of the Cistercian Order. From our own personal resources and from the royal treasury, we undertake to finance it and support it. We command that its construction be undertaken forthwith, close to Pontoise in

the diocese of Paris. And since this house of prayer is founded in honor of the Queen of Heaven, we decree that it shall be known as the Royal Abbey of Blessed Mary.

Blanche, Queen of France

Queen Blanche passed from this world of trial and tribulation on December 1, 1253, in peace and serenity. Her mortal remains were reverently buried at the aforementioned Royal Abbey of the Blessed Mary, which she herself had founded. But, upon her own instructions given prior to her death, her heart was buried separately from the rest of her body, in the Abbey of Holy Mary of the Lilies, which she also had established.

vi. PRINCESS CATHERINE OF THE VERDANT VALLEY

Princess Catherine was born into an aristocratic and ancient Portuguese family, who had held in their power a certain town and region known as the Verdant Valley for many generations.[26] Since her childhood, Catherine venerated the Virgin Mary, the Mother of God, with the greatest reverence and love.

When she reached her fourteenth year and was residing in Lisbon, she was struck with a very serious illness. The pains caused by this malady were truly horrible. Indeed, it brought Catherine very close to death; so much so that her funeral had already been organized, and a coffin and burial shrouds purchased for her in advance.

But in the midst of Catherine's sufferings and the bitter mourning and sorrow which prevailed in all the household, her nurse—who was deeply devoted to Catherine—visited a certain chapel dedicated to the most holy Virgin Mary. Pouring out an abundance of tears and sighs, she supplicated the Mother of God to protect and preserve the life of her young ward, Princess Catherine. And her efforts in imploring the mercy of this powerful helper and protectress were not in vain. For the Blessed Virgin could not be unmoved by the earnest prayers and heart-felt tears of the nurse. And Catherine, who had been so

---

26 In Latin, *Vallis Viridis*. Presumably this refers to a locality in Portugal, rather than Valverde in Lombardy. As the modern name of this place has not been able to be determined, the Latin name has been translated literally into English.

very close to death, little by little regained her grasp on life. After having been desperately ill for four months, she began to recover and her condition improved drastically.

Nevertheless, the disease which had afflicted her so severely did not leave her entirely, nor was she completely freed from its ill effects. For she continued to suffer from severe paralysis on her left side, which deprived her of the capacity to move about as she pleased. And one of her arms suffered from spasms, such that it would tremble and move itself uncontrollably without her volition. This condition persisted for some nine months. During this time, the very best physicians in Lisbon were consulted, yet none succeeded in bringing her any relief or improvement.

Princess Catherine, in desperation, turned once more in prayer to our Lady, the merciful Mother of all Christians. For she trusted that, indeed, the benefits bestowed by the Blessed Virgin are never incomplete or imperfect, and that she who had saved her from the very jaws of death would also restore her to the fulness of health and to the freedom of unimpaired mobility. So Catherine ordered that she should be taken to a small monastery, which was located in the grounds of her family's palace. The chapel of this monastery was dedicated to the blessed Mary, and a genuine relic of the Mother of God was kept there.

Because of the presence of this sacred relic, the particular sanctity of this chapel was widely known and acknowledged. In fact, there was a continuous stream of people who made pilgrimages there, for reasons of prayer. As Catherine entered the chapel and knelt down in prayer and veneration before an image of the Heavenly Virgin, she happened to overhear the words of a certain old woman, who had also come to that place to implore Mary's intercession and aid. In a passionate and remarkably resonant voice, this woman was supplicating with great fervor and intensity for her sick son to the most merciful of Queens. And the ardor of her words was accompanied by a veritable flood of tears and sighs.

Princess Catherine took the prayer of this elderly lady as her example. Thus did she pray: "O most holy Virgin and Mother of Christ, I doubt not that you are able to bestow upon me the medicine of perfect and complete recovery, if I but have faith in your clemency and power. Just as you have procured healing for so many from your divine Son, I beseech you now to come to my own aid in the piteous plight which I now endure!"

With this supplication and other words of piety and prayer, the princess expressed the deepest needs and desire of her heart to the Queen of Heaven. And—behold!—suddenly the paralysis which had afflicted her so grievously was entirely removed, and her full mobility was restored. Her body, which had been vexed and constricted for so long with the effects of her illness, was now animated with perfect liberty. And Catherine was amazed and astounded, her mind raised up in an ecstasy of joy and gratitude!

No longer needing anyone to help her, the young princess stood up and rushed, on agile feet, to her mother who was also in the chapel. She stood before her overcome with waves of happiness, displaying her newly recovered mobility. Her noble mother, as well as all present in the chapel, were quite stupefied at this unexpected and wondrous thing. "A miracle! A miracle!" they all exclaimed with astonishment and reverence.

When the monks of the monastery heard of this amazing wonder and saw that there was no doubt as to its veracity, they gave thanks to the immortal God and his holy Mother, singing the 'Te Deum' with exuberant joy. On the next day, the priests of the community celebrated a Mass of thanksgiving which was attended by the whole household of the palace. And Princess Catherine was joyfully present amongst them, standing easily without the aid of a staff or a servant to support her—something she had been unable to do for the past nine months.

And the healing which the Blessed Virgin had imparted to her was so potent that not only did she have full and perfect mobility, but had also acquired extraordinary strength and endurance in her limbs. Clear evidence of this was in the practice of the princess of praying on her knees every morning. For from the first rising of the sun until eleven o'clock in the morning, she would remain kneeling, without the slightest trace of fatigue or exhaustion.

Catherine's mother, the mistress of the palace, felt such gratitude towards the Mother of God that, from that time onwards, she ordered that whenever there was a feast of the Blessed Virgin it should be observed with the greatest solemnity. Even the servants were released from their usual duties on such days and permitted to partake in the festivities.

The witnesses to the miraculous cure of Princess Catherine included not only the household of the palace, but all the inhabitants of the Verdant Valley and the Carmelite priests who occupied the monastery as well. The story of the miracle spread throughout the entire region, and drew many to make pilgrimages of piety to the Marian chapel there. These pilgrimages continue to this day. And many of those who prayed there have received divine healing and assistance through the intercession of the Mother of God. For truly, the Blessed Virgin loves all those who love her; and, because she loves and adores her own Son, who is the immaculate Lamb of God, she sincerely loves all those who love and believe in him.

Princess Catherine died around the year 1580.

vii. St. Clotilde, Queen of France

St. Clotilde was the wife of Clovis I, the King of France. During the time of his reign, France was graced with a powerful flourishing of the Catholic faith. And Queen Clotilde herself was extremely devoted to the Virgin Mary. Among the many evidences of this devotion was the great convent of nuns which she founded, in honor of the glorious Queen of Heaven.

She also had constructed a wonderful basilica at Les Andelys in the diocese of Rouen in northern France, close to the river Seine. But it happened that all the money which Queen Clotilde had in her treasury ran out and her funds were exhausted. So she found herself unable to pay the many builders, carpenters, stonemasons and artisans whom she had employed to construct the new basilica.

Unable to see any possible solution to the dilemma in which she was now placed, she prayed to the blessed Virgin for assistance. And, miraculously, it was discovered that when any of the workers on the basilica drew forth water from a certain spring fed by the nearby Seine, it was not water at all, but fine wine of a marvelous clarity and richness![27] Not only were they entirely satisfied with this rare and precious wine in lieu of cash payment of their usual ages, but were greatly encouraged in their work in honor of our Lady.

---

27 There is to this day in Les Andelys a spring know as St. Clotilde's Fountain where this miracle is said to have occurred. The waters of this spring are believed to possess miraculous healing properties.

Queen Clotilde left this world of time and space to enter the eternal Kingdom of Heaven in the year of Our Lord 532 (or, according to others, 553), on the third day of June. She is universally venerated as a saint,[28] and her feast is kept on this date not only in France but throughout the entire Catholic world.

---

28 St. Clotilde is the patron saint of queens, widows and brides.

viii. Queen Clotilde of the Goths

Clotilde was the youngest daughter of Clovis I, King of France, and his wife the queen, who was also called Clotilde and whose holy life and ardent piety towards Mary have been described in the previous chapter. This younger Clotilde was married to Amalaric, King of the Goths. But it was far from a happy union. For, whereas Clotilde was of the Catholic faith which then illuminated France, her husband Amalaric was a follower of the dark heresy of Arianism, which still prevailed amongst the Goths.[29] Although the marriage had begun as a promising alliance between the two kingdoms and families, very soon Clotilde began to suffer very greatly at the hands of her non-Catholic spouse.

Eventually, it happened that the unfortunate Queen Clotilde was compelled to flee from the palace of her husband. The exact cause of this is uncertain: some sources indicate that she was trying to escape Amalaric's tyranny and cruelty towards her, whereas others say she had been falsely accused of adultery. Nevertheless, as she was making her escape, alone and unprotected, she passed through a forest and was there set upon by a pack of wolves, which infested the area.[30]

In a state of extreme fear she turned to Our Lady—towards whom she had always nourished a most profound devotion—in

---

29 The Arian heresy denied the full divinity of Christ. It was then prevalent in some parts of Europe and elsewhere.

30 The Latin text does not specify wolves, but says simply 'beasts'. Describing them as wolves is an editorial interpretation; but seems to be fully justified, given that they are described as attacking her in a group.

prayer, asking that her life be spared from the ravenous ferocity and snarling jaws of the animals which assailed her. Suddenly, the Mother of Mercy appeared before her visibly, surrounded by dazzling glory. She commanded the beasts to desist from their fury, and they instantly obeyed her. In fact, not only did they cease their attacks on Clotilde, but henceforth they became her servants and companions, diligently bringing her food and zealously protecting her.

The wolves kept her safe and sound until her brothers came and found her. For these brothers had heard of the cruelty of Amalaric and come from France to rescue their dear sister. They fought bravely against the wicked king of the Goths. Once his forces were overcome and the king himself killed,[31] they took Clotilde back to her homeland of France and returned her to her parents' palace.

In gratitude to blessed Mary, Clotilde had a shrine to her constructed. She also had a wonderful statue carved of the Mother of God, who had so kindly and mercifully preserved her life during her time of peril. This statue was fashioned from pure and incorruptible marble and of the most skillful workmanship and artistry imaginable. Originally, it was adorned with ornaments of gold and precious stones, but—alas!—these have disappeared over the centuries. This statue of the Queen of Mercy is now kept at the convent at Mount Salvation in Spain.

It is marvelously life-like in appearance, but rather bigger than actual human size. From the very beginning, it has been graced with many miracles which have been experienced by those who pray in its presence, especially the healing of diseases.

Clotilde, Queen of the Goths, died around the year 526.

---

31 According to St. Isidore of Seville, Amalaric was killed by his own soldiers.

ix. St. Cunigunde, Empress of the Holy Roman Empire

St. Cunigunde was the wife of the Holy Roman Emperor, St. Henry II; but, with the agreement of her husband was able to maintain a vow of perpetual virginity which she had made prior to her marriage, and both man and wife chose to live in undefiled chastity for the glory of God and the sanctification of their souls. Cunigunde had a profound and loving devotion to the Blessed Virgin Mary, and through her intercession was even able to walk barefoot over red-hot coals.

This came about because her husband, Henry, though normally a good and holy man, was influenced by the promptings of the devil and thus infected with the malign venom of envy. And so he came to suspect Cunigunde of having an amorous affair with a certain soldier. As a way of testing her innocence, he compelled her to walk over a pit filled with burning coals, some fifteen feet in length.[32] As she set her feet upon these, she prayed thus to the Mother of God: "O blessed Mary ever-Virgin! You know well that I have kept myself inviolate and pure, not only from the touch of my husband, but from all other men as well. Accordingly, I beseech you to preserve me now as I pass through this ordeal!" And the voice of the Queen of Angels was heard from Heaven addressing her, "My daughter Cunigunde! I know you are indeed a virgin, just as truly as I am a Virgin. Be assured that I shall save you from all peril and preserve you from all harm!" And so, walking forth bravely, Cunigunde passed over

---

32 Such forms of 'trial by ordeal' were a common practice at this point in the Middle Ages.

the expanse of the red-hot coals on her bare feet, completely unharmed and with perfect serenity.[33]

The same Empress Cunigunde, after the death of her husband the Emperor Henry, had a convent established with the name of Our Lady of Refuge. Saying farewell to all the luxuries and prestige she had enjoyed during her former royal life, she entered this convent herself as a nun on the first anniversary of her husband's passing. There she lived out her days in an exemplary life of devout simplicity and prayer.

St. Cunigunde died around the year of Our Lord 1030, as Baronius[34] relates in his notes to the Roman Martyrology for the third day of March.[35] May she intercede for us all in Heaven!

---

33 Apart from this one unfortunate incident, her marriage to St. Henry appears to have been happy. Since they had both made a vow of perpetual virginity, they did not have any children. Conrad II, a distant relative of Henry II, was elected as his successor.

34 Caesar Baronius (1538-1607), a prominent ecclesiastical historian, and author of the famous *Annales Ecclesiastici.*

35 The feast day of St. Cunigunde.

x. Blessed Dorothea of Prussia

Blessed Dorothea of Prussia was born adorned both by the highest nobility of blood and lineage and the most radiant merit of virtue. It is therefore fitting that she should be accorded an exalted rank amongst Mary's illustrious daughters.

From the age of seven she adopted the custom of fasting on bread and water alone each Saturday, in honor of the Blessed Virgin. This practice she continued to observe diligently for the remainder of her life.

After she had been married for some time, her husband passed away and she was left a widow. Following the example of many other pious women, she then departed from the domestic security of her household and homeland and embarked on a long pilgrimage. She garbed herself in the poor and rough clothes of a wanderer, and made her way to Aachen[36] to visit the celebrated image of the Blessed Virgin there.

As she made her arduous journey on foot, often the Mother of God and various angels and saints would appear to her, offering her words of consolation for the loss of her husband, as well as kindly encouragement for her pilgrimage. The result of these mystical visions was that the desire to serve God was inflamed more and more fervently in Dorothea's heart.

Spiritually fortified, from that point onwards Dorothea led a life of great simplicity and austerity. During the depths of winter—which is bitterly cold in those far northern regions— she would be clad only in a simple cotton tunic. Nevertheless, the ardent flames of divine love which burned within her heart

---

36 A town near Cologne.

sufficed to keep her entire body warm, as if it were a mild summer's day! But when it was summer and the weather was hot, the same internal fire of charity continued to glow within her to such an extent that she was completely unperturbed by the heat of the air which surrounded her.

Once, on the feast of St. Agatha after she had received the Blessed Sacrament, she was caught up in an ecstasy of divine contemplation, her heart feeling the sweet wound of love and celestial desire. Then Christ suddenly appeared to her in a vision, together with his most holy Mother and many other saints. He held five arrows in his hand, and these he affixed firmly but gently into Dorothea's heart. And the Savior said to her, "My beloved daughter Dorothea, for you I bore my five holy wounds of love! Now you, for love of me, shall henceforth bear within your heart these five precious wounds."

As Dorothea approached the end of her life and lay dying on her sick bed, Christ and the Blessed Virgin appeared to her once again. On this occasion both Jesus and Mary gently nursed and fed her with their own hallowed hands.

Blessed Dorothea left this passing and transitory world on September 11, 1399, her loving and pious soul flying joyfully forth to the unending splendors of Heaven.

xi. Countess Ermesinde of Bardenbourg

Ermesinde, Countess of Bardenbourg[37] and daughter of the Grand Duke Henry I of Luxembourg, was graced with a tremendous devotion to the holy Mother of God since her earliest years. This she maintained faithfully throughout her life with many acts of piety, and found therein an unfailing source of consolation and guidance.

She possessed a very ancient but beautiful castle in Bardenbourgh. It happened that one afternoon, for recreation, she had gone out by herself for a stroll in the surrounding countryside. She came across a spring of water near the base of a certain mountain. As she was somewhat exhausted from her walking, she stopped to rest by the spring, seating herself under the cool shade of a large oak which grew there. And as she rested she fell into a light doze, in which she witnessed a most marvelous vision.

For a woman of miraculous beauty and of an awe-inspiring majesty and grace appeared before her. And she held within her arms a small infant, from whom radiated an ineffable aura of goodness and power. This infant was (to use the words of the Psalmist), "more beautiful than the sons of mortals."[38] The woman stood by the spring of water, and as she remained there, a great multitude of small birds began to surround her. Some of them perched upon her arms and her shoulders, while others flew about her lovingly. All of them sang in dulcet tones, their mellifluous and intricate strains pouring forth with sparkling

---

37 In the Wallonia region of Belgium.

38 Psalm 44.2.

vivacity and energy. And the singing of the birds seemed clearly to serve as a hymn of praise to this venerable woman and her divine Son. Both the infant Christ and the Mother of God, in return, looked upon these small birds with happy affection and tenderness.

Ermesinde did not recognize the birds as being of any variety with which she was familiar. Each one had glossy black plumage, extending from its neck downwards, and covering the middle of its back as well as the middle portion of its front. But the rest of the body of each bird was covered with feathers of purest white.

The vision continued for some time, until Ermesinde eventually awoke from her slumber. She then wondered greatly upon the significance of what she had witnessed in her dream, for it had been of such vividness and life-like clarity that she could not doubt that it was sent to her by God himself to convey some message to her. But as to its exact meaning, she was left bewildered.

There was, however, a certain venerable hermit who dwelt in solitude in a small cell in a nearby forest. His reputation for sanctity and wisdom was very great, and he was deeply revered by all the people of the region. So the Countess betook herself to visit this holy man in his cell, making the journey on foot through the dense forest until she found him. He was immersed in divine contemplation at the time, but he greeted Ermesinde warmly and courteously, as if he had been expecting her.

She conversed with the hermit for some time, describing to him in detail the vision which she had witnessed. After praying intently to God for illumination and insight, the anchorite spoke thus, "My Lady, the vision which you have seen is indeed true and trustworthy, and was given to you by almighty God in order to reveal his will to you. By this vision, God is telling you that he wishes you to found, at that very location, a monastery of the Cistercian Order. There, a chorus of holy nuns shall serve and glorify the divine infant who was both Son of God and Son of Mary. They shall also revere and venerate unceasingly the beautiful and gracious woman you say, who was clearly none other than blessed Mary, the Queen of Heaven and the Empress of angels! As for the flock of small birds you saw and heard singing so harmoniously and devoutly, they undoubtedly symbolize the multitude of nuns. For their distinctive plumage, of black upon white, betokens the holy habit of the Cistercian Order. For, as you know, the monks and nuns of that order—the spiritual sons and daughters of the great St Bernard—wear a habit consisting of a white tunic, overlaid with a scapula of black."

The meaning of her vision having thus been explained to her, Countess Ermesinde responded to this divine request with all obedience and alacrity. From her own treasury, she funded the construction of a beautiful convent in the location of the spring of water, where she had seen her vision of Mary and Jesus. This convent was duly consecrated to the glory of God and the honor of his Virgin Mother. Until the present time, this monastery continues to flourish, under the name of the Abbey of Notre-Dame de Clairefontaine, the French word *Clairefontaine* meaning 'clear fountain'.[39] For even today, the clear and sparkling spring of water at which Ermesinde saw her wondrous vision of Our Lady and Christ being venerated by a multitude of small birds continues to flow forth, in the gardens of the convent. And many generations of Cistercian nuns, adorned with the black and white habit of their order, have sung praises to Jesus and his blessed Mother in that place.

The miraculous properties of the water from spring at Clairefontaine are well attested, with a great many healings

---

39 This Abbey is located about two miles from the Belgian city of Arlon close to the border of Luxembourg. Today, it continues to house a flourishing community of Cistercian nuns.

having occurred for those praying at this spring or drinking from its crystalline waters. There is also, at the same convent, an ancient painting of the scene of Ermesinde and her vision of Mary, Jesus, and the distinctively plumaged birds. It is said that if anyone who is afflicted by temptation, anxiety, or despair approaches this painting and looks upon it, whatever sorrows and troubles which have been vexing them are instantly dispelled.

The Countess Ermesinde departed from this mortal life in the year of Our Lord 1216;[40] but she now lives on, both in the eternal life of the Kingdom of Heaven, and in the loving memory of the community of holy nuns at the venerable Abbey of Notre-Dame de Clairefontaine.

---

40 Other sources give 1247 as the year of Ermesinde's death.

xii. St. Galla, Aristocrat of Imperial Rome

I cannot omit from our company of noble daughters of Mary a certain aristocratic woman of Imperial Rome, the holy and faithful St. Galla. As St. Fulgentius, Bishop of Ruspe, testifies in his letter addressed to this illustrious lady, she was the daughter of Symmachus the Consul.[41] Furthermore, her grandfather, father, father-in-law, and son-in-law had all possessed the dignity of being consuls of the Empire as well.[42]

From the very earliest stages of her life, Galla dedicated herself to the veneration of the holy Mother of God, and made Mary her special protectress and guide. And from a young age, she felt a particular awe and reverence towards the Immaculate Conception of Our Lady. Not only did she observe this festivity herself with the greatest possible devotion and joy, but eagerly promoted the doctrine of Mary's sinless and immaculate conception to others throughout her life.

Such was the devotion and piety of Galla towards the Queen of Heaven that Mary, in return, exhibited to Galla the most wondrous graces and benefits. Although but few of these are recorded, there is one in particular which I shall now relate

---

41 St. Fulgentius was Bishop of Ruspe, a city in northern Roman Africa, in the early sixth century. His letters, including the one addressed to St. Galla, are to be found in the *Patrologia Latina* (Volume 65, p. 311).

42 In ancient Rome, the consulate was the highest rank within the political and juridical system. Two consuls were appointed at any given time, and served for a period of one year. To have been chosen as a consul indicated the attainment of the highest social status in the Roman political system.

as having a special prominence in her life's story, and which must surely be accounted as a truly marvelous token of divine grace. In this miraculous event, the elements of nature were transformed and exalted in a stupendous way—as so often is the case with the gifts given by Heaven.

It happened that Galla's husband had passed away, and she was left as a widow. Being of distinguished beauty and noble lineage, naturally there were many distinguished men who eagerly sought her hand in a second marriage. Yet she adamantly refused them all. This was despite the fact that there were a number of considerations which seemed to compel her towards a second marriage, as St. Gregory the Great notes in the fourth book of his *Dialogues*.[43] These included questions of her own safety and financial security and the fact that she was still of nubile age.

Furthermore, there was one very unusual circumstance which afflicted her. Since her widowhood, Galla had begun to grow a beard! Doubtless, this is something which must be counted as a very grave and alarming disfigurement for any woman. And her doctors warned her that unless she should promptly re-enter the married state this unfortunate condition would not stop, but would only become progressively worse.[44]

However, Galla was not concerned with such earthly things, nor with matters of mere external appearance. Rather, her heart and her mind were completely intent upon the glory of God. Each and every day she would take twelve poor beggars into her

---

43 The *Dialogues* of St. Gregory the Great (including the fourth book, from which the story of St. Galla is taken), may be found in the *Patrologia Latina*, Volume 77. The second book of St. Gregory's *Dialogues* is by far the best known of the collection, presenting the earliest life of St. Benedict of Nursia.

44 It seems that the physicians had a primitive notion that the growth of facial hair was due to some chemical or hormonal imbalance, caused by Galla's celibate state as a widow.

house to enjoy a sumptuous lunch, at which she herself would humbly serve.

And it happened that a miraculous image of the Mother of God, holding her divine Son in her arms, was placed in Galla's house by the unseen hands of the holy angels. For this image appeared one morning suddenly and without any other possible explanation. Moreover, it was of incredible beauty and an artistry that surpassed human capacities. It seemed to exhibit the workmanship not of earth but of Heaven. Fashioned out of precious sapphire and spangled with purest gold, it was bathed in a glowing and luminous cloud of iridescent light.

Deeply moved and awe-struck by this marvel, Galla sent news of the wondrous image to the pope, St. John, the first pontiff of that name, who was later to die as a martyr. The pope hastened to Galla's house, and he saw there the miraculous image of Mary. To his astonishment, the glorious icon rose upward, and remained suspended in mid-air. At the same time, all the bells in the city of Rome began to ring together jubilantly of their own accord. After being held high in the air for some time by the angels, the image was gently deposited into the hands of the bewildered pope.

In those days, the people of Rome were afflicted by a devastating plague. But from the time when Pope John had first accepted the image in his hands, the scourges of the plague ceased altogether. A chapel was specially constructed in Galla's palace in which the miraculous likeness of the holy Mother of God was placed, in the location where it had first appeared.

In the *Menologium Benedictinum* of Gabriel Bucelin,[45] under the entries for April 6, he writes:

---

45 This work was first published in 1655.

The illustrious noblewoman of Rome, St. Galla, was a most loving devotee of the Virgin of virgins and the Empress of the Heavens. She lived at the time when the holy Patriarch, St. Benedict, was promoting the Office of the Blessed Virgin. The piety and love of Galla earned for her a special gift from the Mother of God—namely a certain miraculous and beautiful image of her embracing her Son in her arms. This image was fashioned out of precious sapphire and lined with gold, and glowed with a mysterious and brilliant light. When Galla related the news of this wonder to Pope John, he went to her residence and beheld the image suspended in the air by the hands of angels. At that point, all the bells of the city of Rome began to ring spontaneously. The icon was then deposited into the grateful hands of the pontiff. From that time forth, the plague which had been devastating the city miraculously ceased, thanks to the intercession of the Queen of Heaven.

St. Galla died around the year of our Lord 520. May she intercede for all those devoted to the Mother of God, and especially for widows and those separated from their spouses.

xiii. Lady Genovesa of Antwerp

Lady Genovesa, the daughter of the Duke of Antwerp, was the wife of Siegfried, a member of the imperial court and commander in the Emperor's army. In her life and character, Genovesa exhibited a truly praiseworthy example of piety, modesty and patience. Day and night she would devote herself to prayer and contemplation, showing special reverence and love for holy Mary, the Mother of God. Following the evangelical counsels, she would use whatever wealth or possessions were at her own private disposal to give alms to the poor.

The first year of her marriage to Siegfried passed by without her conceiving a child. So she prayed fervently to the heavenly Virgin that she might be granted the blessing of motherhood. And very soon she conceived within her womb, though she herself did not realize it immediately.

At around this same time, her husband was compelled to go forth on a military mission for the Emperor. He also did not realize that his wife was then pregnant. But nevertheless he took all care that Genovesa would be well cared for while he was away. He assured her that, though he would be physically absent, he would always be with her in his heart. He even appointed one of his old and trusted friends, a strong and capable man called Golo, to protect and assist his wife while he was away.

But, alas, how capricious and untrustworthy a thing is human nature! For Golo's loyalty to Siegfried was soon overcome by the allurements of Genovesa's beauty, and the duties of friendship were quickly supplanted by the stirrings of lust. After a short while, Golo ceased merely to guard and protect Genovesa, but began to love her—or, rather, to desire her with the burning impulses of the flesh.

Genovesa was, indeed, of the most exquisite grace and form, such that the heart of any hot-blooded man could scarcely be expected to resist her attractions. Succumbing entirely to his passion, Golo began to try to seduce Genovesa, using compliments, sweet words, gifts, and the customary devices of flattery and blandishments. Yet all his efforts were in vain, for Siegfried's wife remained firmly faithful to her absent husband.

So he restored instead to trickery. He forged a letter with his own hands, purporting to be an official communication from the imperial army. Taking it with him to Genovesa, he said, "Look, my Lady! I have just received this letter, and I think you should read it, though it bears very sad news." When Genovesa read the fraudulent letter, she found it to contain the message that her husband had perished in a shipwreck, together with his whole military unit.

Upon reading this, she was overcome with grief and wept bitterly. She poured forth her anguish and pain in fervent prayer to the Blessed Virgin, in the following words: "O my Lady, Mary ever-Virgin, you alone are my refuge and solace! Look with mercy upon me in my wretched desolation." And, saying this, the Lady Genovesa fainted from sorrow.

And whilst she lay unconscious, the glorious Queen of Heaven appeared to her, enshrouded in radiant light. And she spoke to her sorrowful devotee the following words, "Be strong, my daughter, and take heart! For your husband is not dead; he still lives. Truly, some of his troops have been killed, but Siegfried is still as strong as ever, and unharmed."

As soon as she had heard these reassuring words, Genovesa returned to wakefulness, her former despair quite dispelled. And she called to her servants to bring her some food as refreshment. But the infatuated Golo seized upon this opportunity, and hastened to bring her the tray of food himself. And he said to her, "My Lady—alas!—our common lord and master is dead. As you know, I myself am unmarried. At this point, when the whole power and estate of your late husband seems to fall into my hands and yours, it behooves us to be married and become a couple."

Once he had finished these words, he tried to plant a lustful kiss upon her chaste lips. But Lady Genovesa placed her trust in the assistance of the Blessed Virgin Mary, and punched her would-be suitor in the face as hard as she possibly could! At this, Golo realized that his attempted deception had been discovered, and that his chances of seducing the beautiful Genovesa had entirely vanished. So he hastened away in shame and frustration, together with all his servants and entourage.

By this time, Genovesa was approaching the point of giving birth to her infant. Very soon she delivered a beautiful and healthy boy-child.

And a little while after, her husband, Siegfried, returned from his military expedition, not only alive but quite unharmed. However, the wicked Golo, having been disappointed in his hopes to seduce Lady Genovesa, now sought to take his revenge by accusing her of infidelity during her husband's absence. He asserted that the child she had born was not Siegfried's at all, but the offspring of adultery with some other man. He recommended that she, together with her child, should be drowned, so that all record of the sin should be blotted out. Siegfried very foolishly gave credence to what his trusted friend Golo said, and was enraged at the thought that his dear wife had been unfaithful to him and conceived a child by another man. So he ordered them both to be put to death by drowning, just as the wicked Golo had suggested.

But Genovesa's servants were greatly devoted to her and loved her dearly. So they removed her from the palace secretly, and took her, together with her new-born infant, to a deserted forest where she could escape the anger of her husband. [Then, to make Golo believe that Genovesa had really been executed,] they took the tongue of a dog and gave it to Golo, saying that it was the tongue of their unfortunate mistress.[46]

Genovesa was now left all alone with her child. She wandered through the woods like a second Hagar,[47] sustaining herself and her child with the clear waters of the forest brooks and whatever edible herbs, grasses and berries she could lay her hands upon. During this time she continually resorted to the Virgin Mary in prayer, for consolation and courage to face the difficult conditions under which she was compelled to live.

Living in the forest and eating nothing but the meagre fare that could be gathered from plants, Genovesa found that she was unable to produce sufficient milk from her maternal bosom to feed her baby. Without any human assistance and deprived of all earthly resources, she turned to the Mother of God in humble and desperate supplication, praying, "My Lady, hear the prayer which I, a wretched sinner, pour out to you! As you know, I am innocent of the crime of adultery of which I was falsely accused, and I suffer from a punishment which my actions have not deserved. Do not abandon me, O sweet Mother of God. I know that no one except for you and your only-begotten and divine Son are able to help me and my child now. I beseech you, save my life and the life of my poor son!"

---

46 The Latin text merely states that the servants gave Golo the tongue of a dog, saying that it was the tongue of Genovesa. The only possible explanation of this curious act seems to be that it was intended to serve as proof of her death, and so this has been added into this translation for the sake of clarity.

47 Hagar was the servant of Abraham, who bore him a son, Ishmael. After his wife, Sarah, had conceived, Hagar together with her infant child were driven out into the wilderness. See Genesis 21.

Immediately a voice of heavenly sweetness responded to her, "My beloved friend and daughter, never shall I leave thee!" At once, a female deer came out of the woods and sat before Genovesa's son. It then suckled the infant, as if he were one of her own offspring. This continued to happen, with Genovesa surviving on the herbs and berries she could find, while her baby was sustained and nourished by the milk of the gentle doe.

The mother and her son lived in the forest happily, and a period of some six years and three months elapsed. Then, one year on the day of the Epiphany, her husband, who was out hunting in the woods, chanced to find the two. His former and unfounded wrath towards her had long since abated, and he had come to realize the unblemished fidelity of his wife and to know that the child was truly his own son. With unspeakable joy and relief, the husband and wife were finally united once again!

But Genovesa, in gratitude to the Blessed Virgin, told Siegfried that she would not leave the woods that had been her home for so long, unless he promised to build a chapel to the Mother of God in that place to commemorate the marvelous things that Mary had done for her there. This he did, constructing a small but very beautiful shrine where the Queen of Angels had first appeared to his wife. And at the end of her life Lady Genovesa was buried in this same forest chapel.

As for the cowardly Golo, it happened that shortly after his acts of treachery a herd of four wild oxen set upon him and gored him to death. In this event the words of the Apostle were well illustrated, that "the wages of sin are death".[48]

Lady Genovesa herself died peacefully in about the year of Our Lord 1240.

---

48 Romans 6.32.

xiv. Lady Helen of England

Lady Helen was born of noble and illustrious lineage in the green and pleasant land of England, and was gifted with wealth, status, and beauty. But, alas, she allowed herself to become engrossed in the pleasures and vanities of this passing life. From her early youth until the age of thirty, she drifted into the dark and dangerous paths of sin. Eventually she was reduced to prostitution, in order to maintain her luxurious lifestyle.

In this shameful business which she practiced, she soon became very widely known, for she was, indeed, of remarkable attractiveness. But, not content with her own natural charms, she learned to employ the dark arts of magic and witchcraft. She used these to increase her ability to allure and attract the admiration of others. And, by this means, she accumulated great wealth. Two counts became so infatuated with her that they gave to her their entire estates, in order to gain her favor.

Once, Lady Helen was attending a service in church. She did this not so much out of piety, but out of vanity—that is, to have an opportunity to display her beauty, and to enjoy the admiring looks which she knew she would attract from male members of the congregation. But while she was there, she happened to hear a sermon which was to change her life. The theme of this sermon was the Holy Rosary of the Blessed Virgin Mary, and its immense power as a prayer. Now Helen was deeply impressed by this, particularly on hearing about the effectiveness of this form of prayer. However, she was not actually converted in her heart in any sincere way, but rather felt she could use the Rosary as a means of attaining her own wishes. Indeed, she understood it to be merely another form of charm or spell, whereby she could invoke supernatural powers and employ them for her own purposes. So she found a man who sold Rosary beads, and eagerly purchased a set for herself.

Then, having inquired about the correct method of saying this prayer, she began to recite it systematically and mechanically, as if it were a mere magical formula. At first, of course, her intentions were nothing but the fulfilment of her own personal wishes. Yet after reciting the Rosary for some fifteen days, suddenly a feeling of compunction, which she had never experienced before, sprang up in her heart. She became aware of the sinfulness of her way of life, and she was struck by deep pangs of conscience. This was accompanied by a growing sense of the eternity which awaited her soul, and a dread of the Judgment to come. Eventually, this feeling became so intense and overwhelming that she found herself able neither to sleep, nor eat, nor take her rest.

After continuing with her daily praying of the Rosary, and continuing to endure the anxiety of a guilty conscience, Lady Helen at last resolved to go to confession. There she confessed her sins with the most sincere repentance, openly declaring her faults and failures, and pouring out tears and sighs from the very depths of her heart. Indeed, the priest who heard her confession had never before encountered such sincere and passionate compunction and such an honest and sorrowful admission of guilt.

Once Lady Helen had completed her confession and received sacramental absolution, she knelt in reverent prayer before an image of the Mother of mercy. And then she heard a gentle voice, speaking to her from the image of Blessed Mary. It said, "O Helen, my daughter! Once you were as a ferocious and untamed lioness both to me and to my Son, Jesus. But now you have become an innocent lamb, washing the stain of your sins away with the tears of repentance. How we rejoice that you have entered our sheepfold!"

Overjoyed at this gracious and merciful encouragement, Helen sold all her possessions and distributed the money to the poor. She found a small deserted hut in the woods, and there lived the remainder of her life as an anchorite, devoting herself entirely to prayer, contemplation and works of penance. But, despite the austerity of her life, it was not without its particular delights and sweetness, for she found herself blessed with many spiritual consolations, as well as divine visions and revelations. Very often during the celebration of the Mass, she would see a vision of the living face of Christ in the elevated host. She also found that she could see clearly into the innermost thoughts of all persons whom she encountered.

But her life as an anchorite was not without its challenges. Many times she was vexed by demons, who would endeavor to tempt her and draw her from her commitment to sanctity. But she would always call upon the assistance of the Blessed Virgin. And she proclaimed the 'Our Father' and the 'Hail Mary' to be two precious vessels which contained within themselves the mystery of the Deity. In the contemplative recitation of these prayers, she perceived all that was delightful and beautiful, all that was sweet to the senses and delectable to the mind, and all that filled the heart with ardor and consolation. She described these prayers (the Lord's Prayer and the Angelic Salutation[49]) as being like two radiant lamps which illuminated the hearts and minds of the faithful and led them into the unfathomable and glorious depths of the Trinity. She frequently said that these prayers—like the Blessed Sacrament—bore

---

49 That is, the 'Hail Mary'.

within themselves the very substance of the Divinity, and therefore contained all the splendor of the heavenly court, as well as all the magnificence and beauty of the created world.

Lady Helen's reputation for sanctity and wisdom, and the remarkable story of her conversion through the praying of the Rosary, soon spread through the entire kingdom of England. As a consequence, a great many people adopted this pious practice in emulation of her example.

After a long and dedicated life as an anchorite, when Helen was approaching death, she lay upon her bed with several of her friends and supporters in attendance. And the Lord Jesus Christ together with his blessed Mother appeared to her. As she expired, those present saw her soul ascend visibly from her body, in the form of a dove of radiant whiteness, which flew off into the vault of Heaven. And a fragrance of indescribable sweetness filled the air, while the hearts of all present were filled with the most serene joy—for they realized that their beloved Helen had finally attained admission to that blessed eternity for which she had so long and so fervently yearned.[50]

---

50 No indication of the time when Lady Helen lived is supplied, but given that it was when the Rosary was first becoming popular in England, it seems likely that she lived in the thirteenth century.

xv. Duchess Ida of Westphalia

Ida of Westphalia[51] was born to a family of the highest nobility in her native region, and was given in marriage to the duke, Egbert, who was an intimate friend and honored advisor of the great emperor, Charlemagne.

Ida's beloved husband, Duke Egbert, sadly passed away. A short time after her bereavement, Ida received a vision in which an angel of light appeared before her, robed in garments of dazzling brilliance and surrounded by a cloud of luminous iridescence. The angel spoke, and instructed Ida to build a small but richly ornate chapel in honor of blessed Mary, the Virgin of virgins and the Queen of the Angels.

Once this chapel had been built, the Duchess Ida, now a widow, enclosed herself within its walls. Thenceforth she devoted herself entirely to prayer and meditation, and particularly to the veneration of the Mother of God. And for the rest of her mortal life, she never once set her foot outside the enclosure of this sacred space—having, in effect, already departed from this material world and transcended the realm of time and space to inhabit the eternal dwelling place of divine contemplation. Through her continuous prayers and pious devotion, the holy Duchess sought for nothing else other than to give glory to the Trinity and to venerate the holy Mother of God, with all possible love and reverence.

The admirable and devout Duchess Ida died around the year of Our Lord 800.

---

51 A region of northwest Germany.

xvi. Lady Justina, Countess of Milan

Lady Justina, the Countess of Milan, among other examples of her ardent Marian piety, visited the house of Mary at Loreto[52] and presented there a wondrous altar cloth. This was woven out of thread of gold and silver and finest silk, and fashioned with a certain miraculous and hitherto unseen technique. For the threads of gold, silver and silk were so finely woven that there was not even the space to insert the point of a needle between any of the fibers; and, moreover, it appeared to shimmer and vary itself constantly with an iridescent radiance. It was certainly a work of infinite detail and incredible artistry. Each of the fifteen mysteries of the holy Rosary were depicted upon it with the utmost skill and the finest detail, adorned by images of a seemingly endless variety of flowers, which were so vivid as to seem to be alive.

And, if we believe the reports, Lady Justina not only donated this precious and miraculous masterpiece to the noble House of Loreto, but crafted it with her very own hands. She died around the year 1590.

---

52 This house at Loreto is believed to have been the original home in Nazareth where Mary lived when the archangel Gabriel appeared to her. According to tradition, it was transported by angels to Italy in the late thirteenth century, when the Holy Land was occupied by Muslim forces. The building is made from a kind of stone common near Nazareth, but not found anywhere in Italy.

xviii. St. Lucia, Noblewoman of Compostela

Lady Lucia was born to a family of the highest echelons of the nobility in Compostela in Portugal. She was a sincerely devout girl, and following the example and teachings of the Blessed Dominic, founder and Patriarch of the Order of Preachers, she adopted the practice of diligently saying the Rosary each day from her childhood onwards. When she reached marriageable age, she was united in the sacrament of holy matrimony to a certain distinguished nobleman from the Spanish realm of Granada, and duly took up residence with him in his castle in that warm and sunny region.

But it happened at that time that Islamic forces from northern Africa invaded the Kingdom of Granada, and occupied the land by violent force. Lucia's husband lost his life to the swords of the invaders, and she herself was captured—along with multitudes of others—and sent away into slavery in the distant land of the Moors, in northern Africa. There she was sold into servitude to a barbaric tyrant and forced to work as a slave to his servants, being assigned the most demeaning and lowly tasks imaginable. At this stage, Lucia was already pregnant, carrying within her womb her future son. But her cruel master showed no consideration for her condition, and subjected her to vicious beatings and punishments without mercy.

The months passed by in this manner, and eventually the time for Lucia to give birth arrived. It was then the eve of Christmas. Lucia, in a desperate situation of isolation and without any human companion or helper, took herself off secretly to a stable where the animals slept. In wretched loneliness, her labor commenced. But all the while, she continued to pray the Rosary incessantly, throughout the long vigil of that dismal and painful night. And as she did so, she found the pangs of childbirth to be mysteriously assuaged. For truly the Queen of mercy never fails to come to the aid of her devotees! And in the very early hours of the morning, before the golden light of dawn had dispelled the gloom of night, Lucia gave birth to her child, a tiny son.

But despite the safe delivery of the infant, the anxieties of Lucia were far from over. For in those territories where the Christian faith was not practiced, it seemed that there was little possibility of baptism for the baby. But Mother Mary, together with her divine Son, did not neglect to provide for this also. For suddenly a man robed as a priest appeared. He was of remarkably venerable and compassionate countenance, and his face was suffused with dazzling light. Upon his head there was a crown of thorns, and his hands bore the stigmata of wounds. Yet these were not bleeding, but seemed to shine with the radiance of the stars themselves. He was accompanied by a deacon and a sub-deacon, who bore the waters of baptism and the oil of chrism in a vessel. This priest baptized the child in the name of the Father, the Son, and the Holy Spirit, and gave to him the name of Marianus.[53] The blessed Mary, the Mother of God, was present also. She served as godmother to the child, whom she then took and held affectionately in her arms. The joy and wonder which Lucia experienced upon beholding these things was so great that she completely forgot about the suffering and anxiety she had lately undergone.

Once the baptism had been completed, the Blessed Virgin handed the baby back to Lucia, saying, "Behold—your son! Comfort him and protect him diligently. I myself promise to be with you and him always, and to help you in any need you

---

53 The name *Marianus* means 'Mary-like' or 'Dedicated to Mary'.

may have or peril you may encounter." And with that, the vision disappeared, and Lucia was left alone with Marianus in her arms, in a humble stable housing animals. But Lucia found herself feeling stronger than she ever had before, and animated with a joy beyond all words. She laid her baby in a manger to rest, surrounded by the beasts, in precisely the same manner in which holy Mary had once laid her own Son, Jesus, to rest. And there she remained for forty days, until the feast of the Purification,[54] constantly praising and thanking Christ and the blessed Virgin with the recitation of the Rosary.

On this day, a certain youth with a shining visage appeared to her. He said, "My daughter, because you have not undertaken the customary rites of purification following the birth of your son, you must now prepare yourself to undergo these."[55] Lucia was perplexed and replied, "My lord, there is no church in these parts where I may visit, nor any priest, nor any of the faithful people here either!" The youth replied, "I shall take you to a church of superlative beauty, where you shall see marvels you have never before witnessed, and hear stupendous mysteries you have never before imagined!" And so he led forth Lucia, who carried her son Marianus in her arms, until they came to a miraculous church of a splendor which could hardly be comprehended. There stood Mary Magdalene and St. Anne, the mother of the Blessed Virgin, at the entrance. These took Lucia by her hand, and led her to the choir area.

---

54 February 2.

55 This is a reference to the rites of purification which the Blessed Virgin undertook after the birth of her Son, in accordance with the Mosaic law (see Luke 2.22-39). The text here seems to indicate that it was the practice amongst Catholics at the time to have a Mass or prayers offered forty days after the birth of an infant, in emulation of Mary's purification.

The Queen of Angels herself then appeared to Lucia. She said, "My daughter, often you have presented to me the life and deeds of my own beloved Son through the praying of the Rosary. And so now I shall present you, together with your son, for the rites of purification!"

Then Mary took Lucia by the hand and led her into the chancery of the church, where there was an ornate throne of gold and gemstones, of imperial magnificence. She directed Lucia to sit upon it. And then the mysterious priest, who wore the crown of thorns and bore the radiant stigmata—the same one who had baptized her son—entered, and, with a voice of ineffable beauty and sweetness, sang the holy Mass in dulcet and resonant tones.

When the time for the offertory arrived, the Blessed Virgin gave Lucia a candle, and directed her to present it to the priest. This candle was divided into three portions, from each of which shone forth five dazzling lights. And the candle was of very great size indeed, but was lighter in weight than any usual candle. When it was time to kiss the hands of the priest, a sisterly dispute arose between Mary and Lucia, each contending that the other should have the honor of kissing his hand first. But holy Mary insisted that Lucia should be the first to do so. "For", she said, "this is the day of *your* purification. My own ritual of purification occurred on this same date in the past. It is befitting that you, on this day, should be the first to kiss the divine hands." And so Lucia kissed the hands of the priest—who was clearly none other than Christ himself—first, followed by Mary. And at the end of the holy sacrifice of the Mass, both received communion; again, the heavenly Virgin insisted that Lucia should go before her in accepting the blessed Sacrament.

Lucia was filled with awe and taken up in indescribable ecstasy at the marvelous things she had witnessed and partaken of. The Queen of Heaven then led her by the hand to the door of the church, and said, "My daughter, hold fast to the mysteries and blessings you have received today! Persevere in your holy work of prayer, devotion and the care of your son. And now I shall lead you back to your native land!"

And saying this, with a brilliant flash of light, Lucia suddenly found herself in the Cathedral of San Diego, in her home city of Compostela. And both she and her son, Marianus, continued to dwell in this sacred edifice all the days of their lives, devoting themselves to prayer and contemplation.

After the death of Lucia, Marianus remained as a hermit, dwelling in the Cathedral. His reputation as a man of outstanding sanctity and virtue spread throughout the land. Like his mother, he was particularly devoted to the holy Rosary, and received many visions and revelations.

Lucia passed away around the year of Our Lord 1230, and her son Marianus followed her into the Kingdom of eternal peace in about 1240.

xviii. St. Margaret, Princess of Hungary

Blessed Margaret, daughter of Bela IV, King of Hungary, was filled with the most sincere piety from an early age. This Princess Margaret was to become a maiden of great beauty and exalted status, and consequently her hand in marriage had been keenly sought by the kings of Bohemia, Sicily, and Poland. But she had, from a young age, pledged her virginity, as well as her love and fidelity, to Christ alone—regarding it as more blessed to be the spouse of God himself, than any earthly potentate or prince.

It would be fair to say that she imbibed Marian devotion even as she was nursed as a baby. She had barely reached the age of four when she adopted the practice of the daily recitation of the Office of the Blessed Virgin, chanting the psalms, prayers and hymns with all the diligence of a professed religious. She never once would pass by an image of the Mother of God without kneeling in prayer, and saying a 'Hail Mary'. She often described this as her favorite and most pleasant pastime. Indeed, the holy names of Jesus and Mary were almost constantly upon her lips. On every feast of the Blessed Virgin, and the eight days which followed, she would recite the Angelic Salutation no less than one thousand times—and all of these either kneeling or prostrate upon the ground!

She read the lives of the saints assiduously, and especially those which related miracles concerning Mary. Her own practice was to speak of Mary as "the blessed Hope," or "the Hope of the World," or simply, "the Mother of God."

Her father, the King of Hungary, had a monastery constructed on a certain island in the Danube River, known as the Monastery of the Blessed Virgin. On feast days of the Queen of Heaven, Princess Margaret would abstain from all earthly food, except bread and water alone. Moreover, she listened avidly to sermons preached on this glorious Lady, whom she had chosen as her own particular advocate and helper. And whenever she heard, or uttered, the sacred name of 'Mary', she would kneel in veneration.

The Blessed Virgin did not neglect to respond graciously to this singular devotion offered to her, with remarkable and marvelous demonstrations of her affection and honor. Often, on feast days of the Mother of God, St. Margaret was seen to be raised up off the earth and to be suspended more than a cubit above the surface of the ground, as if both her body and soul were elevated from terrestrial and worldly realities and drawn towards the azure vault of Heaven.

As Margaret approached the time of her death, a great multitude of saints and angels were seen to assemble around her, like a vast and luminous cloud. With great reverence and love, these placed a radiant crown of glory upon her head. And at this time, she saw amongst these celestial beings the Mother of God herself, who began to ascend a ladder reaching from earth and ascending to Heaven. As St. Margaret's soul left her mortal body it followed Mary, her chosen advocate, up this ladder, still bearing the splendid diadem of immortal sanctity which she had received. And thus she passed from this earthly vale of tears to the Kingdom of eternal love and ineffable delight, in the year of Our Lord 1270, on the 28th day of January.

xix. Maria, Duchess of Parma

This Maria was the daughter of the King of Portugal, and the wife of the noble Alessandro Farnese, the Duke of Parma. To express her devotion to the Mother of God, she had constructed a special convent and church dedicated to the Blessed Virgin, under the title of 'Our Lady of Graces'. And she earnestly requested that when her mortal life was over, her body should be laid to rest in this same church. In this way, she declared, her dead body would be protected by the same beloved Virgin who had always protected and guided her so faithfully and lovingly throughout her mortal life.

Duchess Maria's piety in all aspects of the Catholic faith was most admirable, but particularly intense in respect to her devotion to the Queen of Heaven. Such was her love and reverence for the Blessed Mary that she was completely unable to look upon any image of her without instantly falling to her knees in veneration. (The same thing is said also of St. Luke the Evangelist). Now Maria possessed in her palace a beautiful image of the Mother of God. But because she found that she could not look upon it or even walk past it without spontaneously falling to her knees in devotion, she found it necessary to have it covered with a veil. She had the holy image uncovered only when it was possible for her to devote herself entirely to prayer before it, kneeling in supplication.

Maria had, at first, only a single child, a daughter named Margarita. Whilst she was still a small infant, Margarita was afflicted with a grave illness, so severe that the physicians despaired of her life. But Maria turned to the Mother of God in prayer, and shortly thereafter Margarita was miraculously restored to health.

The marriage of Maria and Alessandro was a happy one, but they shared one source of anxiety and disappointment—the fact that they had not been blessed with a male child. On one occasion the couple were together in the Church of Our Lady of Grace, when Maria turned to her husband and suggested they should both pray that, through the intercession of the Queen of Heaven, they should be granted a son. This they did. And nine months later, Maria gave birth to a fine boy-child, whom they would name Duarte, and who became the heir to the family's vast estates and venerable title.

When the end of Maria's life approached, she lay upon her bed with her hands clasped in prayer and her eyes raised to Heaven. She repeated the following verses:

> Mother Mary, quell my fear
> As the hour of death draws near;
> Lead me to eternal bliss,
> There to know thy Son's sweet kiss.
>
> From my sins, O, set me free,
> Guard me from the enemy;
> With a heart, like thine, made pure,
> May I love thee evermore!

Maria, Duchess of Parma, passed from this world to the Kingdom of God in the year of Our Lord 1590.

xx. St. Opportuna, Princess of Osma

S t. Opportuna was born in the town of Osma in Spain, of a noble family closely connected to the royal line. From her early childhood she displayed much clear evidence of her immense devotion towards the Blessed Virgin. It happened that once, when she was a young maiden, she was in church with her parents. She heard the Gospel being proclaimed, and was particularly struck by the words: "Go and sell all that you possess and give the money to the poor, and come, follow me! Then you shall have treasure in Heaven."[56] These words penetrated deeply into the heart of young Opportuna, and she meditated upon them intently and at some length.

After much discernment and prayer, she went to her parents, and humbly fell to her knees before them. She said,

> "Oh, my beloved father and sweet mother, in the awesome and adorable name of the God of Heaven, I implore you not to seek for me any earthly husband. For I desire to have as my spouse none other than the Lord Jesus Christ! I long to follow in the footsteps of Our Lady, the Blessed Mary, the Mother of God. She remained an inviolate virgin forever, and I shall do the same. I will be united in matrimony to the son of no-one, except for the divine Son of her who conceived as a Virgin, who gave birth as a Virgin, and who remains for all

---

56 Matthew 19.21.

eternity a Virgin! Therefore I implore the grace of the Blessed Mother of God that she should accept me as her handmaid, and deign to make me worthy of attending the celestial wedding banquet of her Son. In this way shall I be united to both the Son and the Mother. She shall be my mistress, whilst he will be my Lord and husband. I long for naught else but to serve them both in tranquility for all eternity!"

Opportuna's father and mother were astounded at this outpouring of piety from their daughter. At first they were uncertain how to respond and hesitated for some moments. But they had observed in Opportuna's countenance a certain resolution and heard in her voice an unwavering constancy. Thus they realized it was indeed a divine vocation which motivated her, rather than some passing fancy or ephemeral zeal. Together, her parents gave thanks to God, and prayed that he would bring to full fruition the holy seed which he had planted in their daughter's heart. And all those who were present said, "Amen!"

Upon hearing this, Opportuna was overjoyed. Rising to her feet, she declared,

"Henceforth, I am the daughter of Christ! To him shall I listen; to him shall I incline my ear. Following his teaching, I will strive to forget my own people and the house of my patrimony, for the immortal King of glory has beheld my lowliness, and desired my soul![57] Verily, he is my Lord and God. Him alone shall I adore!"

---

57 See Psalm 44.11-12.

Opportuna quickly took the veil of consecrated life, entering a convent near the city of Sées, in northern France. She chose a convent in such a far distant region so that she would not be recognized by anyone as the daughter of her noble and wealthy family, and so that she would not be given any special treatment or privileges. She united herself heart and soul to this community of devout sisters, who were intent upon serving and glorifying the Lord with great fervor. And, as a nun, she attained to perfect conversion very quickly, and soon became an exemplar of all monastic virtues. So impeccable was her conduct and so sincere was her piety that she never once did anything meriting reproach or requiring correction.

Opportuna lived a life rich in blessings and graces. She was adorned by all virtues, and many miracles and wonders occurred through her prayers. In due course, she was elected Abbess of her community, and was an inspiring and compassionate leader. As the time of her death approached, she was made aware of this by the Holy Spirit. Gathering the sisters to herself, she advised them that in twelve days she was to depart from this passing world. They were greatly saddened, but she offered to them glowing words of consolation and encouragement.

On the night following this, as Opportuna lay in her bed, a great light of dazzling radiance began to shine throughout the whole convent, and a fragrance of indescribable sweetness filled the air. Then Opportuna saw standing by her bed two young and beautiful women, each surrounded by glowing luminescence. She recognized them at once as the virgin-martyrs, St. Cecilia and St. Lucy. "Welcome, my dear sisters Cecilia and Lucy!" she greeted them. "What has our mistress, the glorious Virgin Mary, who is both the Queen of Heaven and the Queen of all virgins, instructed you to tell me?" Answering her, the two saints said, "O most splendid spouse of Christ, blessed Opportuna! Our Mother Mary awaits you in Paradise, so that you may be united in an eternal marriage to her divine Son, whom you have loved and served so faithfully during your earthly life. Adorn yourself now with your crown of glory, and light your lamp, so that you may go forth to meet your Spouse in the unending wedding feast of Heaven!"

Opportuna was filled with overwhelming joy at this blessed vision, and the promise of her approaching celestial union with Christ. Yet she then saw in the corner of her room a demon, small but of terrible appearance. His eyes shone like blazing coals from his horrid visage and gave out fierce sparks, whilst flame issued from his mouth and nostrils. But Opportuna was unafraid, for she knew that this diabolical imp could exercise no power or hold over her. She said to him, "Begone, thou hideous fiend, thou minion of evil! I command thee—get thee hence!" But the demon remained sitting stubbornly where he was.

So the dying saint called all the nuns into her presence in her bedchamber, and told them about the terrible demon which was there. But they could not see him, for he was visible only to Opportuna. Nevertheless, they could smell the acrid fumes which issued from him and sensed his malign presence. Opportuna said to them, "Behold, my sisters, an unclean spirit is amongst us! For such creatures never cease to tempt and vex those dedicated to God. But those who truly make themselves handmaids of the Lord shall unfailingly conquer them. Let us all pray to Christ and his Blessed Mother that this wicked spirit be put to flight." This they did, all praying for a time silently. And by the virtue of their prayer and the power of Christ and the glorious Virgin, the demon was soon overcome, and vanished in a puff of smoke.

After this, Opportuna continued to decline steadily in strength and vitality, and on the twelfth day of her illness, she knew that she would die—as, indeed, she had already foretold to all the sisters. She requested that the sisters arrange for Mass to be celebrated, and that the Blessed Sacrament be brought to her as viaticum for her journey to the next world. This was done, and she accepted the Body of Christ with the greatest love and devotion, saying, "O Lord, may your holy Body profit me for the salvation of my soul!"

After this the nuns remained around her bed, chanting the psalms. Opportuna kept her eyes fixed upon the door of the room, and finally said, "Lo! My mistress, the Blessed Virgin Mary, has at last come for me! My daughters, I commend you all to her care and protection." And she extended her arms, as if embracing the Queen whom she served, and then breathed her last. Thus she left this world to commence her new and eternal life in Heaven as the chosen spouse of her beloved Christ, who lives and reigns with the glorious Father and the life-giving Holy Spirit, God forever and ever. Amen.

St. Opportuna died around the year of Our Lord 770, on the 22nd day of April.

xxi. Princess Philippa a Sylva, of Portugal

Princess Philippa a Sylva was born to the royal family of Portugal, and closely related to the very highest echelons of European reigning families. She was the daughter of Pedro, a Prince of Portugal, and of Isabel, the *Infanta* of Aragon. She was also the sister of Ferdinand, King of Cyprus, and Pedro, King of Aragon and Navarre. However, from an early age she came to hold in disdain all forms of earthly wealth and honor, and sought instead to enter the Kingdom which lasts forever. Accordingly, she entered the Convent of St. Dionysius of the Cistercian Order, located in the region of Odivelas, close to Lisbon, and there accepted the veil of monastic conversion. As a nun, she added to her innate nobility of lineage the marvelous distinction of impeccable sanctity of life.

She was animated in particular by a fervent devotion and profound piety towards the glorious, ever-Virgin Mother of God. It had always been her earnest desire to pass from this mortal life to the Kingdom of Heaven on one of the great feast days of Mary, for she knew that by doing so she would then celebrate that feast with the glorious hosts of angels and saints in her new celestial homeland. And this wish was fulfilled, for she died during first vespers of the Feast of the Purification of the Blessed Virgin Mary, on the first day of February,[58] in the year 1583.

Some time after she had been entombed, the mausoleum which housed her mortal remains was opened, in order to bury

---

58 The feast of the Purification of the Blessed Virgin Mary is February 2. First vespers would have been observed the evening before, i.e. February 1.

one of her cousins who had died. And it was found that Philippa's body was perfectly preserved with no trace of decomposition. But—what is more astonishing—the words of the 'Hail Mary' were found to be inscribed upon her skin (which was still healthy, radiant and unblemished) in many places, in intricate and ornate lettering of a glimmering, unearthly gold! This miraculous phenomena was witnessed and attested to by a great many, who were, naturally, filled with the utmost awe and reverence. Thereafter, Princess Philippa came to be popularly venerated as a saint in her native land, as is recorded by Jorge Cardoso in his wonderful *Agiológio Lusitano*.[59]

---

59 This book, describing the lives of Portuguese saints, was first published in 1652.

xxii. St. Radegunda, Queen of France

St. Radegunda, the daughter of King Bertarius of Thuringia, was the wife of Clotaire I, King of the Franks. She was widely renowned for her sanctity of life and virtues, as well as the innumerable miracles associated with her. In particular, she had an ardent devotion to the holy name of Mary, which even went so far as her having this name tattooed upon her skin. Radegunda carried her love for the Blessed Virgin in her heart, through devotion; she bore it on her tongue, through praise; and she inscribed it onto paper, through composing prayerful books. Furthermore, she also expressed it through her hands, in practical works of charity and piety. For she knew well that without works, all other expressions of faith remain dead.

She observed a 'Marian Lent', which was an annual period of forty days of fasting and abstinence in honor of the Mother of God.[60] Every Saturday—the day sacred to Mary—she would wash and nurse the body of a leper with her own hands. Each Saturday she would also invite some of the poor to her palace to dine, and she herself would humbly serve at the table.

Amongst her special acts of devotion, she had a magnificent church constructed, and dedicated to the holy Virgin. But even as this church was being raised up, she remained conscious of the fleeting and fragile nature of this mortal life, and the uncertainty of the hour of death. She therefore wrote to all the bishops and nobles of France, and had them solemnly swear by the faith of their baptism and under pain of divine retribution, that they

---

60 This was, of course, in addition to the observance of the usual season of Lent, preceding Easter.

would ensure that the basilica was brought to completion if she were to die beforehand. This action seems to have been prompted by some prophetic insight, for Radegunda did indeed die shortly thereafter. But the bishops and nobles of France, obedient to the vows they had made, worked to bring to completion Radegunda's magnificent basilica, which still stands today as a wonderful expression of love for the gracious Maiden who is the Queen of Heaven, the Empress of Angels, and the Mother of God.[61]

St. Radegunda migrated from this earthly life to the glories of Heaven on the 13th day of August, in the year of Our Lord 599.[62]

---

61 This church is today known as the Church of Sainte-Radegonde, in Poitiers, France. It features a remarkable series of stained-glass windows, dating from the thirteenth century, depicting the life of St. Radegunde.

62 Other sources give the year of St. Radegunde's death as 587. A life of St. Radegunde was written by the great Merovingian poet, Venantius Fortunatus, who seems to have also written his most famous hymn, *Vexilla Regis*, at her request.

xxiii. Princess Rosalia of Palermo

St. Rosalia of Palermo was the daughter of Sinibald, the Prince of Palermo in Sicily, and was closely related to the imperial lineage of Charlemagne, the great Holy Roman Emperor. Her aspirations to a life of piety and chastity were so fervent that, at an early age, she left her family's royal palace, and took up residence as an anchorite in a cave on Mount Peregrine, near Palermo. She was led forth to this place of retreat by an angel, and once there, she lived a life of perfect sanctity and holy contemplation.

Princess Rosalia was lovingly devoted to the Virgin Mary, the great Mother of God, and received from her numerous special graces and favors. When she had first contemplated living the life of a hermit, she had turned to the Queen of Heaven and her divine Son in prayer. And these prayers were answered, for both Jesus and Mary imparted to her a special blessing.

She possessed a strand of small beads which she wore on her chest, and frequently used these in her prayers.[63] Once, while she was doing so, an angel appeared to her surrounded by brilliant light. It instructed her in a method of praying using these beads, to Christ and his immaculate Mother. As Rosalia prayed thus with her beads, she would imagine that she was fashioning a splendid crown for the Queen of Heaven.

As a result of the love she offered and the devotion she practiced, on one occasion the Blessed Virgin appeared to her. She bore in her arms her Son Jesus, who had in his hands a

---

63 As Princess Rosalia died in 1160, this was before St. Dominic had popularized the praying of the Marian Rosary.

crown of pure gold. This he gently placed upon Rosalia's head. At another time, the Son of Heaven appeared to her again, as an infant being held in the arms of his Mother, Mary. Numerous angels surrounded him, singing melodies in tones of indescribable sweetness. The venerable apostles St. Peter and St. Paul also stood by in attendance. The infant Divinity was busily fashioning with his own hands a crown woven out of roses and gold. When this was completed, he presented it to Rosalia—as if in return for the very many 'crowns' of prayer she had fashioned for his most blessed Mother.

Princess Rosalia continued to lead her solitary life in her mountain cave, with no companions but Christ, Mary, the angels and saints, as well as her holy beads. She returned her soul to Heaven in peace on the 4th day of September, 1160.

Now, almost five hundred years after Rosalia's death, in the year 1624, a terrible plague was devastating the city of Palermo. It happened that some locals recalled the story of the saintly hermit Rosalia, and hoped that her virtues and prayers might assist them against the pestilence which then prevailed. So they went to search for her dwelling place on Mount Peregrine. By chance (or led by the Holy Spirit), they found her cave, and went inside. There her body was discovered, without the slightest trace of decomposition or decay, but as fresh and radiant as if she were still alive. And she held firmly in her hands her beloved Rosary beads.

Her precious, incorrupt body was then taken to the cathedral at Palermo, and installed there as a holy relic with due and reverent solemnity. Shortly afterwards, the virulent plague which had wrought so much death and suffering suddenly came to an end.

xiv. Princess Salome, the niece of the Queen of England, and Princess Judith, her companion

Princess Salome was born to a royal family, and her mother was the sister of the Queen of England. But while she was still an infant, she was adopted into the household of her uncle and aunt, the King and Queen of all England. And as she grew up, she was of miraculous beauty. Her complexion was such as if the glowing crimson of the blood-red rose were mystically fused with the gleaming and immaculate whiteness of the lily. Indeed, her beauty was such that the hand of no mortal artist could ever create it, nor any human mind imagine it; for it was truly the work of none other than the cosmic Artifex, a refulgent mirror of the celestial splendor of the seraphic courts.

And just as her beauty was so incomparably above all her mortal peers and rivals, so also her heart and soul were far exalted above earthly and material things. She disdained the luxuries, wealth, and comforts pertaining to her royal status, and chose to live as an anchorite, enclosed in a small cell near the Benedictine convent at Augsburg, in Bavaria, known as the Convent of the Ancient Oak.[64] Moreover, she even prayed to Heaven that she might be granted some deformity or disfigurement, lest her physical attractiveness should allure her (or another) into some compromise or violation of her holy chastity. And, lo, her prayer was answered, but in a completely unexpected manner. For

---

64 In German, *Alt-aich.*

Salome was rendered utterly blind, her physical beauty becoming henceforth (at least to her) invisible.

But Salome was consoled by her dauntless faith, and in particular her devotion to the great Mother of God, who is unfailingly compassionate to all who are afflicted. In her hidden cell, Salome lived a life of strict solitude and abstinence, in unceasing contemplation of the glories of Heaven. But in due course, she was joined by another woman of royal blood, Princess Judith, who shared both her contempt for earthly status and wealth, and her bewitching beauty. And together they lived as inseparable, intimate companions in the enchanted seclusion of their forest hermitage for a great many years.

Now, because of her ardent veneration and love for the Queen of Angels, Salome merited to receive a special and miraculous favor from her. For although (as has been noted) Salome was completely blind, whenever a feast day of the Blessed Virgin Mary was celebrated, perfect vision was restored to her for that particular day. And so Salome would be able to see for the duration of the Marian feast, delighting in the golden light of day that was otherwise so sadly denied to her. And it was only on those feast days that she was able to behold the beauteous countenance of her beloved companion, Judith.

Blessed Salome passed from the darkness and misery of this earthly life to behold forever in Heaven the radiant and glorious light of the Supernal Triad, and to contemplate the wondrous and unfathomable beauty of the Empress of the Stars, on the 29th day of June. Her sister in piety and affection, Judith, died some years later, and they were buried together in the same grave— their mortal remains united forever in the narrow confines of the tomb, just as their liberated souls are now surely eternally united in the shoreless and iridescent ocean of celestial, maidenly love.

Unfortunately, to this point, I, the present author, have not been able to discover the year of this most noble lady's death…[65]

---

65 The life of this Princess Salome is recounted only in very brief form by Marracci. Yet she is evidently the same as the St. Salome whose life and legend is recounted in the *Acta Sanctorum* for June 29. St. Salome (who was blind) lived as a hermit together with another woman, St. Judith, in the ninth century. The text above augments Marracci's version with some further details taken from the *Acta Sanctorum.*

'Song of the Stars in Praise of Her'

O starry light of the dim universe!
The night adoreth thee, the planets high
That reign far off within the desert sky
Praise thee as with the sound of dulcimers,
And all the temples of the night rehearse
Thy solemn glory everlastingly!

O thou for whom the moon's pale-lighted star
And all the planets and the milky gleam,
But as a little of thy praising seem,
And the great lights that swim through heaven afar
But the reflection of thy glory are;
Thou only art; these are but shine and dream;

Thou art that light that doth the stars illume,
Thou art the glimmer of the moon divine;
All these are but the garment that is thine;
Thou art the wonder and the glow, the bloom,
Thou art the lonely lamp in night's great gloom,
Thou art the skyey light, the starry shine.

Starlight is but the glory of thy face,
The shimmer of the silver planets pale
Is but the dim effulgence of thy veil;
And the great passing of the nights and days
Is all but as the perfume of thy praise.
O Holy, Holy, Holy; hail, O hail!

David Park Barnitz